Collins

AQA GCSE (9–1)
Maths

Grade 5–7 Booster Workbook

Brian Speed
Helen Ball
David Bird

William Collins' dream of knowledge for all began with the publication of his first book in 1819.
A self-educated mill worker, he not only enriched millions of lives, but also founded a flourishing publishing house. Today, staying true to this spirit, Collins books are packed with inspiration, innovation and practical expertise. They place you at the centre of a world of possibility and give you exactly what you need to explore it.

Collins. Freedom to teach.

Published by Collins
An imprint of HarperCollins*Publishers*

The News Building
1 London Bridge Street
London
SE1 9GF

Browse the complete Collins catalogue at
www.collins.co.uk

© HarperCollins*Publishers* Limited 2019

10 9 8 7 6 5 4 3 2 1

ISBN 978-0-00-832251-9

British Library Cataloguing-in-Publication Data
A catalogue record for this publication is available from the British Library.

Authors: Brian Speed, Helen Ball, David Bird
Expert Reviewer: Trevor Senior
Commissioning editor: Jennifer Hall
Development editor: Joan Miller
In-house editor: Alexandra Wells
Copyeditor: Gwynneth Drabble
Proof reader: Gudrun Kaiser
Answer checker: Deborah Dobson
Cover designers: The Big Mountain Design &
                 Creative Direction
Cover photos: JoeyPhoto/Shutterstock,
              ledmark/Shutterstock
Typesetter: Jouve India Private Limited
Illustrators: Jouve India Private Limited
Production controller: Katharine Willard
Printed and bound by: Grafica Veneta SpA in Italy

The publishers gratefully acknowledge the permission granted to reproduce the copyright material in this book. Every effort has been made to trace copyright holders and to obtain their permission for the use of copyright material. The publishers will gladly receive any information enabling them to rectify any error or omission at the first opportunity.

MIX
Paper from
responsible sources
FSC C007454

This book is produced from independently certified FSC™ paper to ensure responsible forest management.

For more information visit:
www.harpercollins.co.uk/green

Contents

How to use this book

This workbook aims to help you develop the fluency, reasoning and problem-solving skills you need to achieve and reach your full potential in your Mathematics GCSE. It gives you plenty of practice, guidance and support in the key topics and main sections that will have the most impact when working towards grades 5–7.

Each section in this workbook is colour coded as follows: Number, Algebra, Ratio, proportion and rates of change, Geometry and measures, Probability and Statistics.

Question grades

You can tell the grade of each question or question part by the colour of its number:

Grade 5 questions are shown as **1**

Grade 6 questions are shown as **1**

Grade 7 questions are shown as **1**

Use of calculators

You may use a calculator for questions that are marked with a ▦ icon.

> **Hint:** Change each term to a power of 3.

Hint boxes

The 'Hint' boxes provide you with guidance as to how to approach challenging questions.

Revision papers

The three revision papers that are provided in this workbook will help you to prepare for your exams. Papers 1 and 3 do not allow the use of a calculator, but you may use a calculator for Paper 2.

Formulae you should know

You are provided with a list of formulae that you need to know for the examination on pages 149–152.

Answers

You will find answers to all the questions in the tear-out section at the back of this workbook. If you are working on your own, you can check your answers yourself. If you are working in class, your teacher may want to go through the answers with you.

Revision papers

Paper 1 ✂

Name _____ Date _____

1 Express 360 as the product of its prime factors.

_____

_____

_____

_____

_____

(2 marks)

2 Amir is 18 years older than Joy.
Joy is four times as old as Ben.
The sum of their three ages is 72.
Find the ratio of the ages of Ben to Joy to Amir.

_____

_____

_____

_____

_____

_____

_____

_____

(4 marks)

142   Revision papers

1 Number

1.1 Rounding and limits of accuracy ✗

1 Write the smallest number that rounds to:

a 200 _150_   b 53 _52.5_

2 Write the largest number that rounds to:

a 8 _8.5_   b 61 _61.5_

3 Bags of pasta each have a mass of 500 grams, to the nearest gram.
What is the largest possible mass of 10 bags?

_500.5 × 10 = 5005_

4 $A = 58$, $B = 17$. Both values are rounded to 2 significant figure.

a Work out the smallest possible value of:

_57.5 + 16.5 = 74_

_57.5 − 16.5 = 57.5_

i $A + B$ _~~74~~_   ii $A - B$ _40_

b Work out the largest possible value of: _58.5 + 17.5_

_58.5_
_17.5_
_41.0_

i $A + B$ _76_   ii $A - B$. _~~40~~ 42_

5 A number, x, is rounded to 2 decimal places. The result is 3.65

a What is the smallest possible value of x? _____

b What is the largest possible value of x? _____

6 A number, y, is rounded to 2 significant figures. The result is 3.2

a What is the smallest possible value of the reciprocal of y?

Give your answer to 4 decimal places.

_____

_____

b What is the largest possible value of the reciprocal of y?

Give your answer to 4 decimal places.

_____

_____

7 Given that $x = 3.7$ correct to 1 decimal place and $y = 0.55$ correct to 2 decimal places, find the error interval for:

> Hint: The error interval for a rounded value shows the smallest possible value to the largest possible value, e.g. length, h cm, which is 4.2 cm rounded to 1 decimal place has the error interval $4.15 \leqslant h < 4.25$.

a $x + y$ _____ **b** $x - y$ _____ **c** xy _____

8 A rectangle measures 5 cm by 4 cm. Both measurements are correct to 1 significant figure.

a What is the smallest possible area of the rectangle?

_____

_____

_____

b What is the largest possible area of the rectangle?

_____

_____

_____

9 A bridge has a height restriction of 5.03 metres.

A driver knows that his lorry has a height of 5 metres, to the nearest centimetre.

Which of the following statements is definitely true? Give a reason for your answer.

A: The lorry will pass under the bridge.

B: The lorry will not pass under the bridge.

C: It is not possible to tell if the lorry can pass under the bridge.

_____

_____

_____

_____

1.2 Prime factors, LCM and HCF ✗

1 Express 100 as the product of its prime factors.

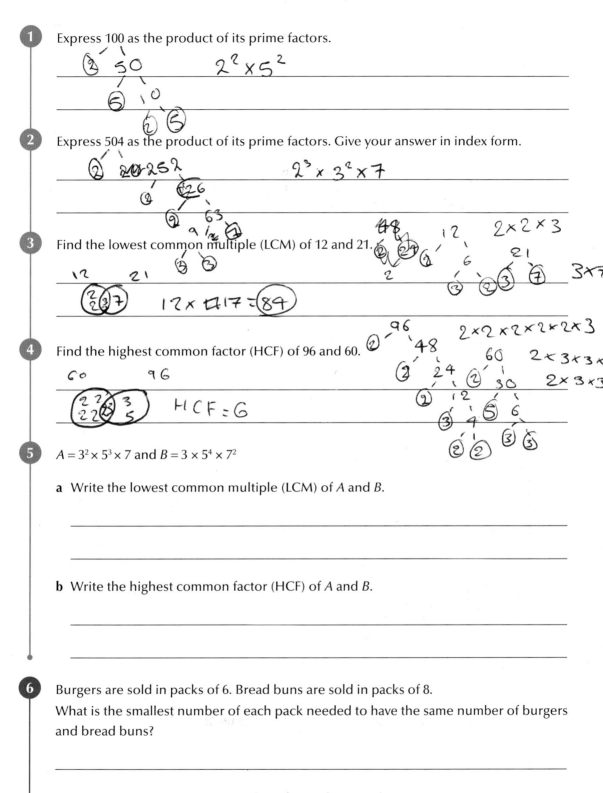

② 50 $2^2 \times 5^2$

⑤ 10

② ⑤

2 Express 504 as the product of its prime factors. Give your answer in index form.

② 252 $2^3 \times 3^2 \times 7$

②

② 63

9 7

③ ③

3 Find the lowest common multiple (LCM) of 12 and 21.

12   21

② ③ 7 $12 \times 17 = 84$

48   12 $2 \times 2 \times 3$
② 24 ④   21
2   6   ② ③ ⑦ 3×7
② ② ③ ⑦

4 Find the highest common factor (HCF) of 96 and 60.

60   96

2 2 2 3
2 2 2 3 5   HCF = 6

96    $2 \times 2 \times 2 \times 2 \times 2 \times 3$
② 48   60 $2 \times 3 \times 3 \times 5$
② 24   ② 30 $2 \times 3 \times 3 \times 5$
② 12   ② 15
③ 4 ⑤ 6
② ② ③ ⑤

5 $A = 3^2 \times 5^3 \times 7$ and $B = 3 \times 5^4 \times 7^2$

a Write the lowest common multiple (LCM) of A and B.

b Write the highest common factor (HCF) of A and B.

6 Burgers are sold in packs of 6. Bread buns are sold in packs of 8.
What is the smallest number of each pack needed to have the same number of burgers and bread buns?

7 Eve does a large shop every 4 days, her mum does a large shop every 9 days, her gran does a large shop every 24 days.

Work out the number of days in a year that they do a large shop on the same day.

_____

_____

_____

_____

8 The LCM of two numbers is 90.

The HCF of the same two numbers is 15.

What is the product of the two numbers?

_____

_____

_____

_____

1.3 Indices, roots and surds

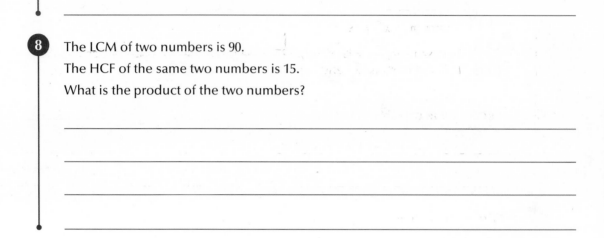

1 Write the value of:

a 5^0 _____ 1 ✓

b 8^1 _____ 8 ✓

c 7^3 _____ 343 ✓

d 5^{-1} _____ $\frac{1}{5}$ ✓

e 4^{-2} _____ $\frac{1}{4^2}$ ✓

f 10^{-3} _____ $\frac{1}{10^3}$ ✓

> **Hint:** Remember $x^{-n} = \frac{1}{x^n}$

2 Write each of the following as a single power of 7.

a $7^2 \times 7^3$ _____ 7^5 ✓

b 7×7^3 _____ 7^4 ✓

c $7^{-2} \times 7^5$ _____ 7^3 ✓

d $7^5 \div 7^3$ _____ 7^2 ✓

e $7 \div 7^3$ _____ 7^{-2} ✓

f $7^{-2} \div 7^5$ _____ 7^{-7} ✓

3 Between which two integers does the cube root of 300 lie?

_____ 6 and 7 ✓

_____

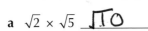

$\sqrt{10}$ $\cancel{\sqrt{20}}$ $\sqrt{50}$ $\cancel{\sqrt{20}}$

$\sqrt{48}$
$\sqrt{16} \times \sqrt{3}$

4 Write each of these square roots in their simplest surd form.

  a $\sqrt{2} \times \sqrt{5}$ ___$\sqrt{10}$___   **b** $\sqrt{10} \times \sqrt{5}$ ___$5\sqrt{2}$___   **c** $\sqrt{8} \times \sqrt{6}$ ___$4\sqrt{3}$___

  d $\sqrt{12} \div \sqrt{6}$ ___$\sqrt{2}$___   **e** $\sqrt{12} \div \sqrt{18}$ _____

5 Find the value of:

  a $36^{\frac{1}{2}}$ ___6 ✓___   **b** $27^{\frac{1}{3}}$ ___3 ✓___   **c** $169^{-\frac{1}{2}}$ ___$\frac{1}{13}$ ✓___

> **Hint:** Remember $x^{\frac{a}{b}} = (x^{\frac{1}{b}})^{a}$.
>
> For example, $9^{\frac{3}{2}} = (9^{\frac{1}{2}})^{3} = 3^{3} = 27$. Always take the root part first as it makes the number smaller and easier to deal with.

6 Find the value of $125^{\frac{2}{3}}$.

_____

_____

7 Write each of the following as a single power of 6.

  a $(6^{2})^{3}$ ___6^{6} ✓___   **b** $(6^{3})^{4}$ ___6^{12} ✓___   **c** $(6^{-1})^{-3}$ ___6^{3} ✓___

8 Simplify each of the following.

  a $\sqrt{24}$ ___$2\sqrt{6}$ ✓___   **b** $\sqrt{18}$ ___$3\sqrt{2}$ ✓___   **c** $\sqrt{180}$ ___$6\sqrt{5}$ ✓___

9 $9^{\frac{1}{5}} \times 3^{x} = 27^{\frac{1}{4}}$

Find the exact value of x.

$\sqrt{(4 \times 6)}$ $\sqrt{4} \times \sqrt{6}$
$\cancel{} = 2\sqrt{6}$

$(3^{2})^{\frac{1}{5}} \times 3^{x} = (3^{3})^{\frac{1}{4}}$ $\frac{2}{5} + x = \frac{3}{4}$

$3^{\frac{2}{5}} \times 3^{x} = 3^{3/4}$ $\frac{2}{5} - \frac{3}{4} = x$

$\underbrace{0.4 - 0.\cancel{7}5}_{} = 0.35$

> **Hint:** Change each term to a power of 3.

10 Solve the equation $2^{x+4} = 1024$.

_____

_____

_____

1.4 Fractions and mixed numbers

(handwritten working at top right:)
$$\frac{4}{8} \quad \frac{5}{10} \quad \frac{8}{16}$$
$$12 \quad 15 \quad 22$$
$$16 \quad 20 \quad 30$$
$$\quad 25$$
$$20 \quad 30$$
$$24$$

1 Work out each of the following. Give each answer in its simplest form and as a mixed number where appropriate.

> **Hint:** In parts **a** and **b**, work with the integers first, then the fractions, before combining to obtain the answer.
> In part **c**, convert each mixed number to an improper fraction first.

a $3\frac{1}{4} + 4\frac{2}{5} - 2\frac{7}{8}$

(handwritten working:)
$$\frac{13}{4} + \frac{22}{5} - \frac{23}{8} \qquad \frac{130}{40} + \frac{176}{40} - \frac{115}{40} = \frac{191}{40} \quad 4\frac{31}{40}$$

$$\begin{array}{r} 40 \\ 80 \\ 120 \\ 160 \\ \hline 200 \end{array}$$

b $5 - 2\frac{3}{5} - 1\frac{3}{4}$

c $3\frac{3}{5} \times 1\frac{4}{21} \times 2\frac{1}{2}$

2 A litre bottle of water is used to fill two glasses: one holds one-third of a litre and the other holds three-eighths of a litre. What fraction of a litre remains in the bottle?

3 Theo lost $\frac{3}{4}$ of his money in a market, but then found $\frac{3}{5}$ of what he had lost.

He now has £21. How much did he start with?

4 Zahar has $12\frac{1}{2}$ litres of lemonade. Glasses each hold $\frac{5}{16}$ of a litre.

How many glasses can he fill from the $12\frac{1}{2}$ litres of lemonade?

_____

_____

_____

5 A miller produces 140 kg of ground rice in a full day. The miller works for $3\frac{1}{2}$ days.

The ground rice is packed into bags with a mass of either $2\frac{1}{4}$ kg or $1\frac{1}{2}$ kg.

One week he fills 185 of the smaller bags. How many of the larger bags can he fill?

_____

_____

_____

_____

_____

1.5 Standard form

> **Hint:** A number is written in standard form as $A \times 10^n$, where $1 \leqslant A < 10$ and n is an integer.

1 Write 6.53×10^{-3} as an ordinary number.

0.00653

2 Work out each of the following. Give your answers in standard form.

a $(7 \times 10^5) + (5 \times 10^4)$ $700000 + 50000 = 750000$ 7.5×10^5

b $(8 \times 10^7) - (3 \times 10^5)$ $80000000 - 300000 = 7.97 \times 10^7$

c $(5 \times 10^6) \times (3 \times 10^4)$ $5 \times 3 = 15 \times 10^{10}$ 1.5×10^{11}

d $(1.2 \times 10^8) \div (4 \times 10^3)$ 1.2×10^{11} $1.2 \div 4 = 0.3 \times 10^5$ 3×10^4

3 The mass of one electron is 9.2×10^{-28} grams.
What is the mass of eight million electrons?

$8 \times 10^6 \times 9.2 \times 10^{-28}$ 73.6×10^{-22} 7.36×10^{-21}

$8 \times 9.2 = 73.6$ $-28 + 6 = -22$

4 One grain of sand has a mass of 2.5×10^{-3} grams. How many grains of sand are in a bag of sand with a mass of 1 kg? Give your answer in standard form.

$1000g \div 2.5 \times 10^{-3}$

5 The table shows some information about some of the planets in our solar system.

	Distance from the Sun (miles)	Diameter (miles)
Earth	9.3×10^7	7.9×10^3
Mars	1.3×10^8	4.2×10^3
Mercury	3.6×10^7	3.0×10^3
Uranus	1.9×10^9	3.2×10^4
Venus	6.8×10^7	7.5×10^3

a Which of these planets is the closest to the Sun?

b What is the difference between the diameters of Uranus and Mars?

c Kim said that the further away the planets are from the Sun, the greater the diameter. Is she correct? Give a reason for your answer.

6 A reservoir contains 1.9×10^8 litres of water. During some dry spell weather, the volume of water in the reservoir reduced by 1.3×10^6 litres each day.

a The dry weather lasted 5 weeks. How much water was in the reservoir after these 5 weeks?

b If the dry spell had continued, how many more days would it be before the reservoir was empty?

1.6 Recurring decimals to fractions

1 Draw a line from each number on the left to its equivalent 6 significant figure number on the right.

0.101	0.101 010
0.10$\dot{1}$	0.101 111
0.1$\dot{0}$$\dot{1}$	0.101 101
0.$\dot{1}$0$\dot{1}$	0.101 000

2 Write these numbers in order of size. Start with the smallest.

0.73$\dot{5}$ 0.7$\dot{3}\dot{5}$ 0.$\dot{7}$3$\dot{5}$ 0.735

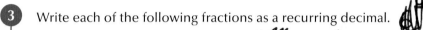

0.735   0.7$\dot{3}\dot{5}$ 0.73$\dot{5}$ 0.$\dot{7}$3$\dot{5}$

3 Write each of the following fractions as a recurring decimal.

a $\frac{1}{3}$ _____   **b** $\frac{1}{6}$ ~~0.16~~ $0.1\dot{6}$ **c** $\frac{5}{6}$ _____

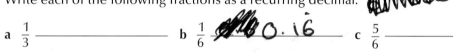

4 Write these numbers in order of size. Start with the smallest.

0.88   0.$\dot{8}$ $\frac{4}{5}$ 0.888

_____

5 Sam said: 'You can write one-third as a terminating decimal.' Show that she is **not** correct.

_____

_____

_____

6 Convert each of these recurring decimals to a fraction in its simplest form.

> **Hint:** To convert 0.$\dot{8}$ to a fraction, start by writing $x = 0.8888...$; hence $10x = 8.8888...$ then you can subtract to find the value of $9x$.

a 0.$\dot{2}$

$10x = 2.22222$
$x = 0.22222$
$9x = 2$
$x = \frac{2}{9}$

b 0.$\dot{5}\dot{4}$

$100x = 54.545454$
$x = 0.545454$
$99x = 54$
$\frac{54}{99}$ $\frac{6}{11}$

7 Javid said that the answer to 0.$\dot{6}$ × 6 is 4. Show that he is correct.

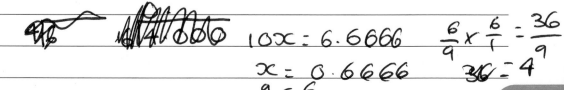

$10x = 6.6666$
$x = 0.6666$
$9 = 6$

$\frac{6}{9} \times \frac{6}{1} = \frac{36}{9}$
$36 = 4$

2 Algebra

2.1 Factorisation

1. Factorise each expression.

   > **Hint:** Remember the difference of two squares.

   a $t^2 - 1$ $(t+1)(t-1)$ **b** $w^2 - 64$ $(w-8)(w+8)$ **c** $x^2 - 36$ $(x+6)(x-6)$

2. Factorise each expression below the hint.

   > **Hint:** Remember to look for factor pairs of the constant term to help you to find the coefficient of x.
   > For example, to factorise $x^2 + 5x + 6$, consider the factors of 6: 6×1 and 3×2; only one pair (3 and 2) will give factors that sum to 5, hence the factorisation is $(x + 3)(x + 2)$.

   a $x^2 + 7x + 12$ $(x+3)(x+4)$ **b** $x^2 + 8x + 12$ $(x+2)(x+6)$ **c** $y^2 + 2y - 24$ $(y-6)(y+4)$

3. Factorise each expression.

   a $4x^2 - 9$ _____   **b** $16 - x^2$ _____   **c** $25x^2 - 4$ _____

4. Factorise each expression.

   a $x^2 - \dfrac{1}{4}$ _____   **b** $y^2 - \dfrac{1}{16}$ _____   **c** $4t^2 - \dfrac{1}{9}$ _____

5. Factorise each expression.

   a $x^2 - 18x + 32$ **b** $x^2 - x - 72$ **c** $x^2 - 8x + 16$

   _____   _____   _____

   _____   _____   _____

   _____   _____   _____

6. This is Ben's solution to the factorisation of $15x^2 - 2x - 1$:

   $15x^2 - 2x - 1 = (5x - 1)(3x + 1)$

   He has made a mistake.

   Correct his mistake.

   _____

   _____

   _____

7 Show that $n^2 + 3n + 2$ is an even number for all integer values of n.

_____

_____

_____

_____

2.2 Setting up and solving linear equations ✗

1 Eve and Fred are making bookmarks.

Each hour Fred makes 8 more than Eve makes.

In 2 hours they make 64 bookmarks altogether.

a Let x be the number of bookmarks that Eve makes in an hour.

Set up an equation in terms of x.

_____

_____

_____

b Solve your equation to find the value of x.

_____

_____

2 A regular pentagon has side length $(2x + 1)$ cm.

An equilateral triangle has side length $(4x - 1)$ cm.

The pentagon and the triangle have the same perimeter.

Work out the value of x.

_____

_____

_____

_____

$2x \; 2(x-3)(x+3)$

$5(x-9)(x+9)$

3 A number, n, is divided by 2 and the answer is added to the same number, n, divided by 3.

The answer is 10.

What was the starting number, n?

_____

_____

_____

_____

4 24 is subtracted from a number, n. The result is the same when n is divided by 3.
Work out the value of n.

_____

_____

_____

5 Theo takes 30 minutes to drive from home to work one morning.

He takes 20 minutes to drive home, when his average speed was 20 km/h greater than when he was going to work.

Work out the average speed at which he drove home.

_____

_____

_____

_____

6 The diagram shows an isosceles triangle. All measurements are centimetres. Show that the area of the triangle is 12 cm².

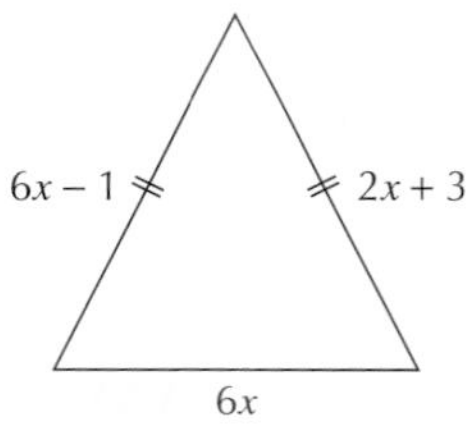

_____

_____

_____

_____

_____

_____

_____

$6x - 1$ $\quad$ $2x + 3$

$6x$

7 Dylan jogs at 9 km/h along a road. He then walks back along the same road at 7 km/h.

He takes 1 hour altogether.

Work out the total distance covered.

Give your answer to 1 decimal place.

_____

_____

_____

_____

2.3 Solving quadratic equations by factorising

1 Solve the following quadratic equations.

a $x^2 + 10x + 24 = 0$

_____

_____

_____

_____

b $x^2 + 9x + 20 = 0$

_____

_____

_____

_____

c $x^2 + x - 6 = 0$

_____

_____

_____

_____

c $x^2 - 6x + 5 = 0$

_____

_____

_____

_____

2 Kiera and Andrew both solved the quadratic equation $x^2 - 25 = 0$.

Hint: Remember the difference of two squares.

Kiera solved it by factorisation, but Andrew said he had solved it in a different way.

a Show how Kiera solved the equation.

_____

_____

b Show how Andrew may have solved the equation.

_____

_____

3 Solve the following quadratic equations.

a $2x^2 - 5x - 3 = 0$

b $3x^2 + 4x + 1 = 0$

c $20x^2 + 11x - 3 = 0$

d $6x^2 - x - 1 = 0$

4 Solve the following quadratic equations.

a $4x^2 - 25 = 0$

b $25x^2 - 9 = 0$

c $25 - 16x^2 = 0$

d $9x^2 - 0.01 = 0$

5 Tia solved the quadratic equation $x^2 + 3x + 2 = 0$ by factorising, but her solution is incorrect.

$$x^2 + 3x + 2 = 0$$

$$x^2 + 2x + x + 2 = 0$$

$$x(x + 2) + 1(x + 2) = 0$$

$$(x + 2)(x + 1) = 0$$

$$x = 2 \text{ or } x = 1$$

Where is/are her mistake/s?

6 Solve the following quadratic equations.

a $6x^2 + x = 2$

b $8x^2 + 15 = 22x$

7 The length of a room is 4 metres greater than its width.

Hint: Let the width be x m and the length be $(x + 4)$ m.

The area of the floor is 221 m².

Work out the dimensions of the room.

2.4 Solving quadratic equations by completing the square

1 Show that $x^2 + 8x - 3$ is equivalent to $(x + 4)^2 - 19$.

2 Nav is given this question.

Solve the quadratic equation $x^2 - 6x = -5$ by completing the square.

Here is his solution.

$(x-3)^2 - 9 = -5$

$(x-3)^2 = 4$

$x - 3 = 2$

$x = 5$

a Correct his mistakes.

b Use another method to solve the quadratic equation $x^2 - 6x = -5$.

_____

_____

_____

3 Write each expression in the form $(x + a)^2 + b$, where a and b are constants.

a $x^2 + 6x + 4$ **b** $x^2 - 18x - 2$ **c** $x^2 - 4x + 1$

2.5 Changing the subject of a formula

1 Rearrange each of these formulae to make t the subject.

> **Hint:** Make sure you show each step of your working.

a $A = mt + 5$

$-S \qquad -S$
$A - S = mt$
$\div m \qquad \div m$
$\frac{A-S}{m} = t$

b $k = wt^2$

$\div w \qquad \div w$
$\frac{k}{w} = t^2$
$\sqrt{\frac{k}{w}} = t$

c $H = \dfrac{5t - 3}{4}$

$\times 4 \qquad \times 4$
$4H = 5t - 3$
$+3 \qquad +3$
$4H + 3 = 5t \div 5$
$\div 5 \quad \frac{4H+3}{5} = t$

d $p = \dfrac{8}{t - 1}$

$\times t - 1 \qquad \times t - 1$
$pt - 1 = 8$
$+P \qquad +P$
$pt = 9$
$\div p \quad t = \frac{p+8}{p} \div p$

e $m = \dfrac{t + 1}{t}$

$mt = m - 1 = \frac{t}{t}$

f $k = 4t^3$

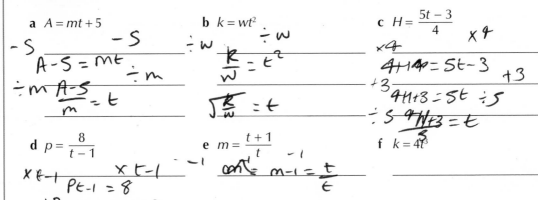

2 Make r the subject of each of these formulae.

a $A = 4\pi r^2 \div 4\pi$

b $V = \frac{4}{3}\pi r^3 \quad \times 3$

$\times 3$
$3V = 4\pi r^3 \quad \div 4\pi$
$\div 4\pi \quad \frac{3V}{4\pi} = r^3$
$\sqrt[3]{\frac{3V}{4\pi}} = r$

c $k = 2\pi\sqrt{\dfrac{r}{w}} \quad \div 2\pi$

$\div 2\pi$
$\frac{k}{2\pi} = \sqrt{\frac{r}{w}} \quad 2$
$\frac{k^2}{4\pi^2} = \frac{r}{w} \quad kw$
$\times w \quad \frac{kw^2}{4\pi^2} = r$

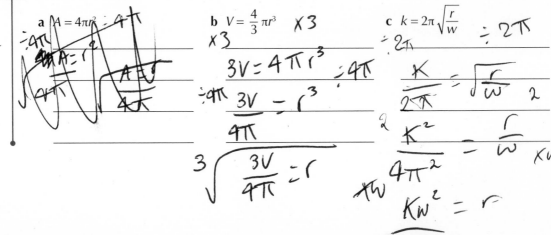

3 Make v the subject of each of these formulae.

a $E = \frac{1}{2}mv^2$

$\div 0.5$ $\div 0.5$

$\dfrac{E}{\frac{1}{2}} = mv^2$

$\div m \dfrac{E}{\frac{1}{2}m} = v^2 \quad \sqrt{}$

$\sqrt{} \sqrt{\dfrac{E}{\frac{1}{2}m}} = v$

b $d = \dfrac{mvk}{3}$

$\times 3$ $\times 3$

$3d = mvk$

$\div k \dfrac{3d}{k} = mv \div m$

$\div m \dfrac{3d}{km} = v$

c $t = a + \dfrac{v-1}{d}$

$\times d$ $\times d$

$td = a + v - 1$

$+1 \quad td = a + v$ $+1$

$-a \quad td - a = v$ $-a$

4 This is Eve's solution to change the subject of a formula to x. She is incorrect.

$y = \dfrac{18(w-x)}{x}$

$yx = 18w - x$

$yx - x = 18w$

$x(y-1) = 18w$

$x = \dfrac{18w}{y-1}$

a Where did Eve make her error(s)?

_____

_____

_____

b Correct her answer.

_____

_____

_____

5 Make x the subject of each of the following formulae.

a $5x + y = 8 - 3x$

_____

_____

_____

_____

b $3(x + 2y) = 5x - 3$

_____

_____

_____

_____

c $m(x + p) = q(x - t)$

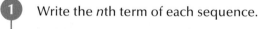

_____

_____

_____

2.6 Using the *n*th term to generate sequences ✖

1 Write the *n*th term of each sequence.

> **Hint:** Look at the sequences of the numerators and the denominators separately.

a $\dfrac{1}{3}, \dfrac{3}{5}, \dfrac{5}{7}, \dfrac{7}{9} \ldots$

_____

b $\dfrac{5}{8}, \dfrac{8}{12}, \dfrac{11}{16}, \dfrac{14}{20} \ldots$

_____

c $\dfrac{4}{100}, \dfrac{9}{95}, \dfrac{14}{90}, \dfrac{19}{85} \ldots$

_____

d $-\dfrac{2}{5}, -\dfrac{6}{12}, -\dfrac{10}{19}, -\dfrac{14}{26} \ldots$

_____

2 This sequence of patterns is made from wooden sticks.

Pattern 1   Pattern 2   Pattern 3

a Draw pattern 4 in this sequence.

b How many sticks would you need for the nth pattern of squares in this sequence?

_____

c What is the largest pattern you could make with 120 sticks?

_____

_____

3 Given that $U_n = 5n - 3$, Nav works out that the first five terms in the sequence U_1, U_2, U_3, U_4, U_5 are –3, 2, 7, 12, 17. Explain what is wrong with Nav's answer.

_____

_____

_____

4 Given that $U_n = 10 - 3n$, Hannah works out that the first five terms in the sequence U_1, U_2, U_3, U_4, U_5 are 7, 4, 1, –1, –4. Explain what is wrong with Hannah's answer.

_____

_____

_____

5 Write the nth term of each of these sequences.

a 100, 91, 82, 73…   **b** 0.9, 0.8, 0.7, 0.6…

_____   _____

_____   _____

_____   _____

6 Here is a sequence.

$$\frac{1}{11}, \frac{\sqrt{2}}{12}, \frac{\sqrt{3}}{13}, \frac{1}{7}, \frac{\sqrt{5}}{15} \dots$$

Hint: See if you can make the numerators and the denominators belong to sequences.

Show that the 100th term in this sequence is also $\frac{1}{11}$.

_____

_____

_____

7 Circle the expression for the nth term of the sequence

−5, −2, 1, 4

$3n + 2$ $\qquad\qquad$ $3n - 8$ $\qquad\qquad$ $8 - 3n$ $\qquad\qquad$ $3n - 2$

8 Here is a linear sequence:

$4, 1, \frac{6}{9}, \frac{7}{13}, \frac{8}{17} \dots$

Show that the product of the 17th and 18th terms is $\frac{28}{299}$.

_____

_____

_____

2.7 Linear inequalities ✗

1 Write the inequality that represents the values of x that satisfy both of these inequalities.

$-3 \leqslant x \leqslant 5$ and $0 \leqslant x \leqslant 10$

_____

_____

2 Given that $2 \leqslant x \leqslant 9$ and $-5 \leqslant y \leqslant 3$, work out:

a the largest possible value of $x + y$

_____

_____

b the smallest possible value of $x^2 + y^2$.

_____

_____

3 Write all the possible values of x such that x is a prime number and $11 < x < 50$.

_____

_____

_____

4 On the grid, shade the region that satisfies all the inequalities below the hint.

Hint: Draw the lines first and then decide which side of the line satisfies each condition.

$y \geqslant 2$ (1)

$x + y \leqslant 7$ (2)

$y \leqslant 3x$ (3)

Label the required region R.

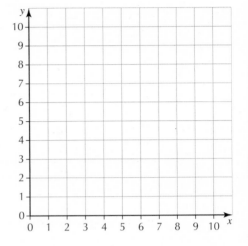

5 Solve the following inequalities.

a $3x + 5 > 2$ **b** $4t - 7 \leqslant -5$ **c** $\dfrac{x}{2} + 1 \geqslant 3$

_____   _____   _____

_____   _____   _____

_____   _____   _____

2.8 Finding the equation of a straight line

Hint: Make sure you show each step of your working.

1 A straight line passes through the points $(1, 5)$ and $(4, 17)$.

a Work out the gradient of the line.

_____

_____

b Work out the equation of the line.

_____

_____

2 The straight line L is shown on the grid.

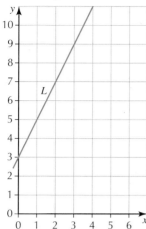

Work out an equation for line L.

_____

_____

3 Work out the equation of a straight line that:

a has gradient 3 and passes through the point (4, 5).

_____

_____

_____

b passes through points (1, 1) and (4, 7).

_____

_____

_____

_____

4 Work out the equation of the line that is parallel to $y = 3x + 8$ and passes through point (3, 4).

_____

_____

_____

5 The grid shows the line AB. OA is 8 cm, OB is 4 cm.

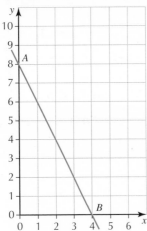

a Write the gradient of AB.

_____

b Write the equation of the line AB.

_____

_____

6 Show that the points A(–2, 1), B(1, 2) and C(7, 4) are all on the same straight line.

_____

_____

_____

_____

7 Lucas is finding the equation of the line with gradient –2, passing through the point (4, 3). His answer is $y = 11 + 2x$. Is he correct? Give a reason for your answer.

_____

_____

_____

2.9 Drawing quadratic graphs and using them to solve equations

1 **a** Complete this table of values for $y = 3x^2 + 2x - 4$.

x	−2	−1	0	1	2
y	4		−4		

b Draw the graph of $y = 3x^2 + 2x - 4$ on the grid below, for values of x from −2 to 2.

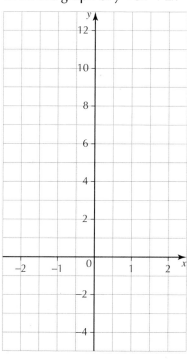

c An approximate solution of the equation $3x^2 + 2x - 4 = 0$ is $x = 0.87$

Describe how you can find this solution from the graph.

_____

_____

d Use the graph to find another solution to $3x^2 + 2x - 4 = 0$.

_____

2 The diagram shows the graph of $y = x^2 - 3x + 2$ for values of x from -1 to 4.

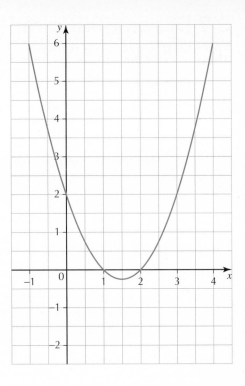

a Describe how to find the solution to $x^2 - 3x + 2 = 6$ from the graph.

_____

_____

_____

b Use the graph to find the solution to $x^2 - 3x + 2 = 6$.

_____

3 This is a graph of $y = x^2 - 2x - 5$ for values of x from -2 to 4.

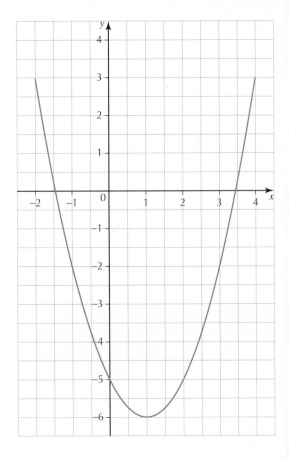

a Use the graph to solve the following equations.

  i $x^2 - 2x - 5 = 0$

  _____

  ii $x^2 - 2x - 5 = 3$

  _____

b Ben said he could solve the equation $x^2 - 2x - 7 = 0$ by drawing a straight line on the grid.

  i Write the equation of the line that Ben would need to draw.

  _____

  ii Use this line to solve the equation.

  _____

2.10 Recognising the shapes of graphs

These are sketches of the graphs in questions **1** to **9**.

A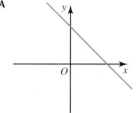

B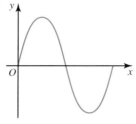

C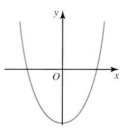

D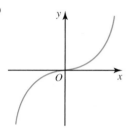

E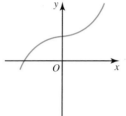

F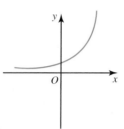

G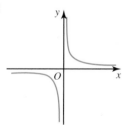

H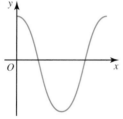

I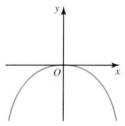

Match each equation to its graph.

1 $y = x^3$ is graph _____

2 $y = \dfrac{1}{x}$ is graph _____

3 $y = x^2 - 4$ is graph _____

4 $y = -x^2$ is graph _____

5 $x + y = 7$ is graph _____

6 $y = x^3 + 4$ is graph _____

7 $y = \sin x$ is graph _____

8 $y = 2^x$ is graph _____

9 $y = \cos x$ is graph _____

2.11 Trigonometric graphs

These are the graphs of $y = \sin x$ and $y = \cos x$ for $0° \leqslant x \leqslant 360°$.

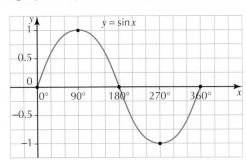 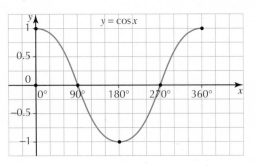

1 Use the graphs to find the value of:

a sin 0°   **b** sin 90°   **c** sin 270°

_____   _____   _____

d cos 0°   **e** cos 90°   **f** cos 180°

_____   _____   _____

2 Dan said, 'Between 0° and 360°, there are two angles that have a sine of 0.5.' How can you use one of the graphs to show that this is true?

_____

_____

_____

3 Sam said, 'The sine of 45° is the same as the cosine of 45°.' How can you use the graphs to show that this is true?

_____

_____

_____

4 Use your calculator and the graphs above to help you find the solutions to the following equations. Give your answers to the nearest degree within the interval 0° to 360°.

> **Hint:** Make sure your calculator is in degree mode.
> Use the symmetry of the graphs to help you to find the solutions.

a sin x = 0.8031   **b** sin x = –0.4123

_____   _____

c cos x = 0.5476   **d** cos x = –0.0811

_____   _____

2.12 Simultaneous equations

1 Solve each pair of simultaneous equations.

a $5x + 3y = 1$
$2x - 3y = 13$

_____

_____

_____

_____

_____

_____

b $5x + y = 0$
$3x - 2y = 13$

_____

_____

_____

_____

_____

_____

c $2x + 3y = 29$
$3x + 2y = 16$

_____

_____

_____

_____

_____

_____

2 4 teas and 3 coffees have a total cost of £13.80.

2 teas and 5 coffees have a total cost of £15.30.

Work out the cost of 1 tea and the cost of 1 coffee.

_____

_____

_____

_____

_____

_____

3 Max is attempting to solve the following equations.

$8x + y = 7$

$6x - 2y = 41$

This is his attempt:

$$8x + y = 7 \quad (1)$$
$$6x - 2y = 41 \quad (2)$$

From equation (1): $\qquad\qquad y = 7 - 8x$

Substitute into equation (2): $\quad 6x - 2(7 - 8x) = 41$

$$6x - 7 + 8x = 41$$
$$14x = 49$$

Substitute into equation (1). _____

Solution $x = 3.5$ and $y = -21$ _____

He has made two mistakes. _____

What are the mistakes?

4 In ten years' time, David will be twice as old as his daughter. Ten years ago he was 6 times older than she was. How old are they now?

> Hint: Let David's age now = x and his daughter's age now = y.
> Set up two equations with two unknowns and solve.

_____

_____

5 Solve this pair of simultaneous equations graphically.

$y = x^2$ $y = 3x + 5$

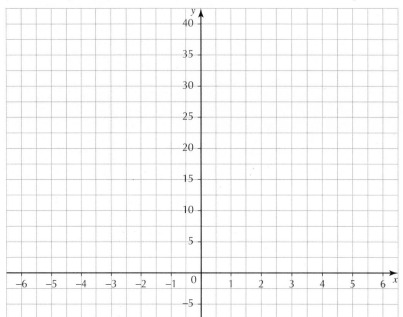

2.13 Equations of circles and their graphs ✖

1 **a** Complete this table of values for $x^2 + y^2 = 4$.

x	−2	−1.5	−1	−0.5	0	0.5	1	1.5	2
y		±1.3		±1.9		±1.9	±1.7		

b Give a reason why there are generally, but not always, two values of y for each value of x.

_____

_____

c **i** Draw the graph of $x^2 + y^2 = 4$ on the grid on the right.

   ii Write the radius of the circle.

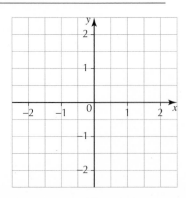

2 a Draw the graph of $x^2 + y^2 = 9$ on the grid on the right.

b Write down the radius of the circle.

_____

3 Dan said, 'The circle with equation $x^2 + y^2 = 16$ has radius 4.'

Explain why this is true.

_____

_____

_____

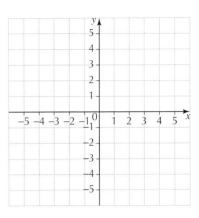

2.14 Working with algebraic fractions

1 Solve each of the following equations.

a $\dfrac{x}{2} + 3 = 7$

b $\dfrac{3x}{4} - 1 = 8$

c $\dfrac{x+3}{5} = 2$

_____   _____   _____

_____   _____   _____

_____   _____   _____

2 Eve is trying to solve the equation $\dfrac{x}{7} - 3 = 1$.

This is her attempt.

$\dfrac{x}{7} = 7 + 3$

$x = 70$

What mistake did she make?

Correct her mistake and work out the correct solution.

_____

_____

_____

3 Solve each of the following equations.

a $\dfrac{2x+1}{3} = 5$

b $\dfrac{3x-1}{4} = 2$

c $\dfrac{x-1}{5} = \dfrac{1}{10}$

_____   _____   _____

_____   _____   _____

_____   _____   _____

4 Solve each of the following equations.

a $\dfrac{1-x}{2} = 2x - 7$

b $3x - 5 = \dfrac{x+1}{3}$

c $x + 3 = \dfrac{x-3}{4}$

_____

_____

_____

5 Omar is trying to solve the following equation.

$$\dfrac{x-1}{3} = \dfrac{2x+1}{5}$$

This is his working.

$3(2x + 1) = 5(x - 1)$

$6x + 3 = 5x - 1$

$x = -4$

He has made a mistake.

What is his mistake?

_____

_____

_____

6 Simplify each of the following expressions.

a $\dfrac{x^2 - x - 2}{x - 2}$

b $\dfrac{x+3}{x^2 + x - 6}$

_____

_____

7 **a** Write an expression for the area of the rectangle.

_____

_____

_____

_____

$\dfrac{1}{x+1}$

$\dfrac{1}{x-1}$

b Find the value of x, given that the area of the rectangle is $\dfrac{1}{3}$ m²

_____

_____

c Write an expression and calculate the value for the perimeter of the rectangle. Give your answer as a single fraction.

_____

_____

_____

2.15 Plotting and interpreting $y = k^x$

1 **a** Complete the table of values for $y = 2^x$.

x	0	1	2	3
$y = 2^x$				

Use these values to draw the graph of $y = 2^x$ on the grid below.

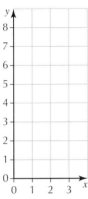

b Use your graph to estimate the solution to $2^x = 6$.

2 Kath has an advent calendar with a bag for each day from 1 December to 24 December. On 1 December she puts £1 into its bag, on 2 December she puts £2 into its bag, on 3 December she puts £4 into its bag.

a Show that you would expect her to put £8 into the bag on 4 December.

_____

_____

b Explain why 2^{10} gives the number of £s into the bag on 11 December.

_____

_____

_____

c How much money should she put into the bag on 24 December?

_____

_____

_____

2.16 Functions

1 The function $f(x)$ is defined as $f(x) = 15 - 2x$.

   a Find $f(3)$ **b** Find $f(-3)$ **c** Solve $f(x) = 0$

_____   _____   _____

_____   _____   _____

_____   _____   _____

_____   _____   _____

2 The function $g(x)$ is defined as $g(x) = 2x^3 + 3$. Find:

   a $g(2)$ **b** $g(-4)$ **c** $g(\sqrt{3})$

_____   _____   _____

_____   _____   _____

_____   _____   _____

_____   _____   _____

3 f and g are functions such that $f(x) = \dfrac{1}{x}$ and $g(x) = 8x^2$.

   a Find $f(-4)$ **b** Find $g(-2)$

   c For what value of x does $f(x) = g(x)$?

4 f and g are functions such that $f(x) = 8 - 2x$ and $g(x) = \dfrac{x - 4}{4}$.

a Find $f(-1)$

_____

_____

_____

_____

_____

b Find $g(-2)$

_____

_____

_____

_____

_____

c Find the value of x when $g(x) = -0.5$.

_____

_____

_____

_____

_____

d Joe said that there is one value of x for which $f(x) = g(x)$. Find this value of x.

_____

_____

_____

_____

_____

3 Ratio, proportion and rates of change

3.1 Simplifying ratios, and ratios as fractions ✗

1 Write each ratio in its simplest form.

a $18:48$ _____   b $63:14$ _____   c $35:90$ _____

d $36:70:12$ _____   e $24:42:66$ _____   f $13:91:41$ _____

2 Draw lines to join each ratio of quantities on the left to its matching ratio in its simplest form on the right.

> Hint: Remember to write each part in the same units first.

a 15 cm to 1.05 m $20:7$

b 1 kg to 350 g $15:7$

c 6 minutes to half an hour $1:7$

d 15 cm to 150 cm $2:7$

e 60 seconds to $3\frac{1}{2}$ minutes $1:5$

f 1.5 kg to 700 g $1:10$

3 The following are the ratios of boys to girls for six classes in a school.

a Class A $7:8$ b Class B $5:6$

c Class C $1:7$ d Class D $4:3$

e Class E $3:7$ f Class F $4:9$

i For each class, work out the fraction that is girls and the fraction that is boys.

> Hint: Remember to write each fraction in its simplest form.

_____   _____

_____   _____

_____   _____

ii What is the minimum number of students there could possibly be in each class?

_____

_____

_____

_____

_____

_____

4 The recipe for 12 cup cakes is 100 g of self-raising flour, 25 g of cornflour, 130 g of caster sugar, 120 g of butter. What is the ratio of butter to sugar to flour?

_____

_____

5 $\frac{3}{7}$ of the marbles in a jar are red. The rest are blue.

a What is the ratio of blue marbles to red marbles?

_____

_____

b Could there be 98 marbles in total in the jar? Give a reason for your answer.

_____

_____

6 The age of a child and the age of her mother are in the ratio 1:8.
The age of the mother and the age of the child's grandmother are in the ratio 6:11.
All the ages are integer values.
What are the possible ages of the child, mother and grandmother?

_____

_____

_____

_____

7 Three children Brad, Max and Dan share a chocolate bar in the ratio 1:2:5.
Dan gets 150 grams more chocolate than Max.

a How much chocolate does each child get?

_____

_____

b Does the chocolate bar weigh more than 350 grams?
Show how you work out your answer.

_____

_____

c Dan eats $\frac{1}{10}$ of his share of the chocolate bar. What is the new ratio of the three children's shares of the remaining chocolate? Give your answer in its simplest form.

_____

_____

_____

_____

3.2 Dividing a quantity in a given ratio ✖

1 Divide each amount in the given ratio.

a 1 kg in the ratio 3:17   **b** 0.6 m in the ratio 9:1   **c** £5 in the ratio 19:6

_____   _____   _____

d 49 cm in the ratio 1:4:2   **e** 1 litre in the ratio 6:9:35   **f** 250 g in the ratio 6:3:1

_____   _____   _____

2 Decide whether each of the following statements is true or false.
If a statement is true write T. If it is false, write F and give the correct answer.

a £7.75 divided in the ratio 3:22 is £0.62 and £7.13.

_____

b 6 hours divided in the ratio 35:37 is 2 hours 55 minutes and 3 hours 5 minutes.

_____

c 1 mile divided in the ratio 1:9 is 167 yards and 1548 yards.

_____

> Hint: Remember, there are 1760 yards in a mile.

d 2 kg divided in the ratio 12:13 is 1040 g and 960 g.

_____

e 4 m divided in the ratio 2:3:11 is 50 cm, 75 cm and 275 cm.

_____

f £1250 divided in the ratio 10:17:23 is 250p, 425p and 600p.

_____

3 On one day, the ratio of ice creams to lollipops sold in a shop was 7:11.
The shop sold 143 lollipops.

a How many ice creams were sold?

_____

_____

b What was the total number of ice creams and lollipops that were sold?

_____

_____

4 Three children share £200 in the ratio of their ages, which are 10, 13 and 17.

  a How much does each child receive?

  _____

  _____

  b The eldest child gives some of his share to the youngest child.

  The eldest and youngest now have the same amount. How much money did he give?

  _____

  _____

5 In Year 7 there are 180 students. The ratio of girls to boys is 2:1.

  In Year 8 there are 160 students. The ratio of girls to boys is 3:1.

  How many girls are in Years 7 and 8 altogether?

  _____

  _____

  _____

  _____

6 Mick is making a cake. He needs flour, butter and sugar in the ratio of 7:8:10.
He needs 240 grams of butter.

  a How much flour and how much sugar does he need?

  _____

  _____

  _____

  b Work out the total mass of the cake before baking.

  _____

  c Work out the amounts of flour, butter and sugar Mick needs, to make a cake $2\frac{1}{2}$ times the size.

  _____

  _____

  _____

  d How much will the cake in part **c** weigh?

  _____

7 Orange paint is made up of 10% of thinner mixed with red paint and yellow paint in the ratio 2:1.

Liz wants to make 2.25 litres of orange paint.

She has:

- 220 ml of thinner
- 1250 ml of red paint
- 680 ml of yellow paint.

a Does she have enough thinner, red paint and yellow paint to make enough orange paint? You must show your working.

_____

_____

_____

_____

_____

_____

b How much orange paint, to the nearest millilitre, could she make with these quantities?

_____

_____

_____

8 Doug, Harry and Kai are brothers.
Doug is 3 years younger than Harry and Kai is five years older than Harry.
Their grandfather is 70 years old. This is twice the combined ages of the brothers.

a How old are Doug, Harry and Kai?

_____

_____

_____

b The brothers are given £280 to share in the ratio of their ages.
How much do they each receive?

_____

_____

_____

3.3 Using ratio 🖩

1 Write each ratio in the form $1:n$. In parts **c** to **f**, give n as an improper fraction in its simplest form.

a $7:28$ **b** $4.5:9$ **c** $18:45$

_____ _____ _____

d $63p:£1$ **e** $2\,\text{hours}:27\,\text{minutes}$ **f** $77\,\text{cm}:1.3\,\text{m}$

_____ _____ _____

2 For each part, work out the value of X, as either an integer or a fraction.

a $11:19$ can be written as $1:x$

_____

b $x:128$ can be written as $1:8$

_____

c $x:24$ can be written as $1:\dfrac{3}{4}$

_____

d $5:17$ can be written as $x:1$

_____

e $x:\dfrac{3}{2}$ can be written as $9:1$

_____

f $x:30$ can be written as $\dfrac{5}{12}:1$

_____

3 The scale on a map is $1:25\,000$.
Jayden uses the following method to work out the ratio in a different form.

$1\,\text{cm}:25\,000\,\text{cm}$ _____

$1\,\text{cm}:250\,\text{m}$ _____

$1\,\text{cm}:2.5\,\text{km}$ _____

$2\,\text{cm}:5\,\text{km}$ _____

Is his answer correct? If not, then rewrite it, correcting his mistake.

4 Anna and Mike share a snack. They share the snack in the ratio $5:3$.
Anna gets 80 grams more than Mike.

a How much of the snack does Mike have?

_____

_____

b How much did the snack weigh in total?

_____

_____

5 a The required ratio of teachers to students on a school trip is 1 : 8.
What is the ratio of teachers to students, in the form n : 1?

_____

_____

b Fifty-three students are going on a school outing.
How many teachers are needed to accompany the students?

_____

_____

_____

c What is the maximum number of students that could drop out so that only six teachers are required?

_____

_____

_____

6 The scale on a map is given as 1 : 50 000. The scale on another map is given as 1 : 25 000.
a How many centimetres are there to a kilometre on each map?

_____

_____

_____

_____

_____

_____

b What length, in kilometres, would be represented by 5 cm on each map?

_____

_____

_____

_____

7 Maggie is paid £17 000 per annum after tax and national insurance.
She pays £5200 per annum in rent.
Of the rest, she puts a quarter into her savings account, and spends 30% on food.
She spends a third of the remainder on going out, and the rest on clothes.

a What is the ratio of savings to food to going out to clothes?

_____

_____

_____

_____

_____

_____

b What is the ratio of rent to savings to food to going out to clothes?

_____

_____

_____

_____

_____

_____

_____

She decides to increase the amount that she puts into her savings account by 10%,
and takes this amount from the money she previously spent on clothes.

c What is the ratio of savings to food to going out to clothes now?

_____

_____

_____

_____

_____

_____

_____

3.4 Best-buy problems 🔲

1. In each part, compare the unit prices and state which item is the better value.
   a Apples at £1.60 for 5 or £2.25 for 6

   _____

   _____

   b Dishwasher tablets at £7 for 58 or £12 for 72

   _____

   _____

2. In each part, compare the unit prices and state which item is the best value.
   a Toilet rolls at £1.80 for 4, £3.35 for 9 or £6.50 for 16

   _____

   _____

   b Shampoo at £3 for 250 ml, £4 for 300 ml or £5 for 450 ml

   _____

   _____

3. A shop sells two different types of potatoes: baking potatoes at £2 for 1.75 kg and salad potatoes at 70p for 700 g.
   a Work out the cost per kilogram for each type of potato.
   Give your answers to the nearest penny.

   _____

   _____

   _____

   _____

   b For each type of potato, work out the mass of potato you get for every £1 you spend.

   _____

   _____

   _____

   _____

   c Which type of potato is the better value?
   Use your answer from parts **a** and **b** to state how you made your decision.

   _____

   _____

3 Ratio, proportion and rates of change

4 Compare the prices of each of these shampoo deals. Amanda says that Bossie is the best deal. Is she correct? You must show your working to support your answer.

_____

_____

_____

_____

_____

_____

_____

_____

_____

_____

5 Paul sat three different tests. He scored 35 out of 48 on the first test, 59 out of 80 on the second test and 43 out of 60 on the third test. He claims he did equally well on all three tests. Is his claim correct? You must show your working.

_____

_____

_____

_____

_____

_____

_____

6 A shop sells two types of dog food.

WOOF
100 grams in packs of 12.

**SPECIAL OFFER:
2 PACKS FOR** £6

ROVER
150 GRAMS IN PACKS OF 8.

**SPECIAL OFFER:
2 PACKS FOR** £8

The shopkeeper does these calculations.

Woof: $12 \times 100\,g = 1200\,g$

$2 \times 1200\,g = 2400\,g$

$\frac{2400}{6}\,g = 400\,g$

So £1 buys 400 grams of Woof.

Rover: $8 \times 150\,g = 1200\,g$

$2 \times 1200\,g = 2400\,g$

$\frac{2400}{8}\,g = 600\,g$

Since for £1 I get 600 grams of Rover, then Rover is better value.

Are the shopkeeper's calculations correct? Is Rover better value?

Give reasons for your answer.

_____

_____

_____

_____

7 A runner completes a marathon of 26.2 miles in 3 hours.
A few weeks later she runs a 10K race in 38 minutes.

Hint: A 10K race is a 10-kilometre race. Take 1 mile = 1.6 km.

a Work out the ratio of the number of kilometres run in the marathon to the number of kilometres run in the 10K race.

_____

_____

_____

_____

b In which race was the runner's average speed higher?

_____

_____

_____

_____

_____

_____

3.5 Compound measures ▦

1 Use the relationship between speed, s, distance, d, and time, t, to answer the following questions.

Hint: Use the triangle that links speed, distance and time.

a Pat drives 174 miles in 6 hours. Work out her average speed.

_____

_____

b Becky cycles around the Isle of Wight at an average speed of 15 mph.
The journey takes 5 hours. How far did Becky cycle?

_____

_____

c A racing driver completes one 5900 m lap of Silverstone at an average speed of 64.8 m/s. Work out the time taken, to the nearest second.

_____

_____

2 Complete the table.

	Hours worked, h	Hourly rate, r	Pay, p
a	7 hours	£9.25	
b	8 hours per day for 5 days	£17.85	
c	37.5 hours		£742.50
d	40 hours		£416.00
e		£16.45	£394.80
f		£11.65	£489.30

3 A glass cuboid of mass 115 g has dimensions 2 cm × 4 cm × 6 cm.
Calculate the density of the glass. Give your answer correct to 1 decimal place.

Hint: Use the triangle that links density, mass and volume.

4 In part **a** and **b** of this question, assume that when a person walks in high heels, all of their mass acts through the heel and only one foot is on the ground at a time.

a Assuming that the heel is a circle with a radius of 7 mm, what pressure would a 65 kg person exert? Include the units in your answer.

Hint: Pressure = $\dfrac{\text{force}}{\text{area}}$

b The same person, with a mass of 65 kg, puts on a different pair of high heels. The radius of each heel of the new pair of shoes is 5 mm. What is the percentage increase in pressure from the pressure exerted in part **a**?

_____

_____

_____

_____

_____

_____

_____

c Which of the following statements is correct, when both feet are on the ground at the same time compared to when just one foot is on the ground?

   i The pressure will be higher.

   ii The pressure will stay the same.

   iii The pressure will be lower.

5 A train travels from Norwich to Nottingham. It leaves Norwich station at 09:57. The train travels 118 miles at an average speed of 20 m/s. At what time will the train arrive in Nottingham?

_____

_____

_____

_____

_____

_____

Hint: Take 1 m/s = 2.24 mph

6 **a** In one week, a student works 40 hours. For 29 hours she is paid £5.90 per hour. For the remaining hours she is paid 20% more per hour. How much is she paid that week?

_____

_____

_____

_____

b In the same week, an older student works 40 hours. For 29 hours he is paid £7.28. For the remaining hours he is paid 30% more per hour.
How much more is the older student paid that week?

_____

_____

_____

_____

_____

_____

_____

7 **a** Carbon steel is made in 1 tonne blocks. The density of carbon steel is 7850 kg/m³. What is the volume of a carbon steel block?

Hint: 1 tonne = 1000 kg

_____

_____

_____

_____

b The ratio of the mass of iron alloy to the mass of carbon in the carbon steel is 199:1. The density of carbon is 2.3 g/cm³. What is the volume of the carbon in a 1 tonne steel block?

_____

_____

_____

_____

_____

_____

c What is the density of the iron alloy?

_____

_____

_____

_____

3 Ratio, proportion and rates of change

3.6 Compound interest and repeated percentage change

1 Bank accounts pay either simple interest or compound interest.
For each account, work out if the interest is simple or compound.

a £3000 invested for 3 years at 1.5% gives £137.04 in interest.

_____

_____

b £500 invested for 2 years at 0.75% gives £7.50 in interest.

_____

_____

c £2000 invested for 5 years at 2% gives £208.16 in interest.

_____

_____

d £200 invested for 3 years at 0.85% gives £5.10 in interest.

_____

_____

e £2500 invested for 2 years at 2.5% gives £125.00 in interest.

_____

_____

f £4000 invested for 2 years at 1.75% gives £141.23 in interest.

_____

_____

2 Complete the table for different cars.

	Car start value	Depreciation rate per year (based on value at start of each year)	Number of years	Final value
a	£12 000	10%	2	_____
b	£8 500	20%	3	_____
c	£25 000	2%	7	_____
d	£6 750	9%	4	_____
e	£9 000	12.5%	5	_____
f	£1 000	25%	3	_____

3 When Zac was born, his grandmother invested £100 for him in a bank account with a compound interest rate of 1% per year. How much will there be in his bank account when he is 21 years old, assuming the bank continues to pay interest at the same rate?

_____

_____

_____

_____

_____

4 Ali buys a bike for £1400. Its value depreciates by 5% each year.
After how many years will it have depreciated by over 30%?

_____

_____

_____

_____

_____

_____

5 Mel has £3000 to invest in a bank account for 5 years. In which bank should she invest?

NORTHERN BANK

2% COMPOUND INTEREST FOR FIRST 2 YEARS

0.75% COMPOUND INTEREST FOR NEXT 3 YEARS

SOUTHERN BANK

1.5% simple interest for 2 years

1% simple interest for the next 3 years

Western Bank
1.75% compound interest for 5 years

_____

_____

_____

_____

_____

_____

_____

_____

_____

_____

_____

6 A compound interest rate of 20% is applied to an invested amount each year. After how many years will the original investment have doubled in value?

_____

_____

_____

_____

_____

_____

7 Ben put £1000 into a savings account. The interest rate was compound at 0.65% per year. At the end of X years he had made £53.20 in interest. Show that $X = 8$.

_____

_____

_____

_____

_____

_____

_____

_____

_____

_____

8 In 1960 the population of the UK was 52 433 157 people.
In 1980 the UK population had increased to 56 265 475.

a Show that the percentage growth in the UK population from 1960 to 1980 inclusive was 0.353%, to three decimal places.

_____

_____

_____

_____

_____

_____

From 1980 to 2000 the percentage growth slowed so that by 2000 the population of the UK was 58 950 848.

b If the 1960 to 1980 percentage growth had continued at 0.353%, how much bigger would the UK population in 2000 have been than it actually was?

_____

_____

_____

_____

_____

_____

3.7 Reverse percentages 🖩

1 Decide if each statement is true (T) or false (F).
If a statement is false, write the correct answer.

a 5% is 40, so 100% is 80.

_____

_____

b 60% is 75, so 100% is 105.

_____

_____

c 80% is 520, so 100% is 650.

_____

_____

d 2.5% is £10, so 100% is £400.

_____

_____

e 17.5% is £171.50, so 100% is £805.50.

_____

_____

f 115% is £34.50, so 100% is £23.

_____

_____

2 129 Year 6 students have school lunch. This is 86% of Year 6 students.
Work out the number of students in Year 6.

_____

_____

_____

3 A shop sells an item for £63.60. This includes VAT (value added tax) at 20%.
Show that the VAT is £10.60 on this item.

_____

_____

_____

_____

4 In September, the number of visitors to a tourist attraction was 325.
This is a fall of 35%, compared to August.
Work out the number of visitors to the tourist attraction in August.

_____

_____

_____

_____

5 For her evening job a student has a 3% increase in pay followed by a 4% increase in pay. Her new weekly pay is £160.68. Which of the following calculations correctly works out her original pay? Identify the mistakes in the incorrect calculations.

a £160.68 ÷ 1.03 = £156

£154.50 ÷ 1.03 = £151.46

_____

_____

b £160.68 ÷ 1.07 = £150.17

_____

_____

c £160.68 ÷ 1.04 = £154.50

£154.50 ÷ 1.03 = £150

_____

_____

d £160.68 × 1.04 = £167.11

£167.11 × 1.03 = £172.12

_____

_____

6 The price of a microwave oven increases by 6% to £159.
A customer works out that the price has increased by £9.54. Is he correct?
You must show working to support your answer.

_____

_____

_____

_____

_____

_____

_____

7 Sue puts some money in the bank at 1.5% compound interest per annum.
After 3 years she has £6274.07. How much did she originally put in the bank?

_____

_____

_____

_____

_____

_____

_____

_____

8 Show that an increase of 10% followed by an increase of 30% is the same as an
increase of 43%.

_____

_____

_____

_____

3.8 Direct and inverse proportion 🖩

1 Decide whether each of the following relationships shows direct proportion (D), inverse proportion (I) or neither (N).

a The number of days of rain and the number of umbrellas sold.

_____

_____

_____

b The result in a Mathematics test and the number of photographs taken.

_____

_____

_____

c The number of hours worked and the amount of pay received.

_____

_____

_____

d The number of hours spent on homework and the number of hours of TV watched.

_____

_____

_____

e The number of miles travelled and the amount of fuel left in the tank of a vehicle.

_____

_____

_____

f The number of houses in a village and the number of cars in the village.

_____

_____

_____

2 Draw lines to join each question on the left to its matching answer on the right.

a 12 eggs cost £2.90 in total. What do 18 of the same eggs cost?

_____

£6.50

_____

b 15 bottles of water cost £9.75 in total. What do 10 of the same bottles of water cost?

_____

£14.40

_____

c 7 packets of crisps cost £6.93 in total. What do 3 of the same packets cost?

_____

£4.35

_____

d 5 pizzas cost £9.00 altogether. What do 8 of the same pizzas cost?

_____

£2.97

_____

3 A car uses 22.5 litres of petrol on a 180-mile journey.

a How much petrol will the car use on a 126-mile journey?

_____

_____

The fuel tank of the car holds 60 litres of petrol.

b Work out the distance the car will travel if it uses three-quarters of a full tank of petrol.

_____

_____

c What assumption have you made in parts **a** and **b**?

_____

_____

4 In this question, assume that all servings are of equal size.

Al makes one size of cake that serves 12 people. He uses 225 g of butter in each cake. Al needs to make enough of these cakes to serve 90 people.

a How much butter will he need?

_____

_____

_____

_____

b How many extra people could he serve?

_____

_____

c How many fewer cakes would he need if each cake served 4 more people?

_____

_____

5 S is directly proportional to T. When $S = 30$, $T = 6$.

a Show that $S = 5T$.

_____

_____

_____

_____

_____

b Work out S when $T = 3$.

_____

_____

_____

c Work out T when $S = 100$.

_____

_____

_____

_____

6 P is directly proportional to Q. When $P = 75$, $Q = 15$.
Jen shows this method to work out the equation connecting P and Q.
She has made a mistake. Find and correct the mistake.

$P \propto Q$ _____

$P = kQ$ _____

$15 = 75k$ _____

$k = \dfrac{1}{5}$ _____

$P = \dfrac{Q}{5}$ _____

7 L is inversely proportional to M. When $L = 7$, $M = 4$.

Is it true that when $L = 35$, $M = 0.8$? Show your working to support your answer.

_____

_____

_____

_____

_____

8 Mia can exchange £240 for €300.

a How many euros (€) are there to the pound (£)?

_____

_____

_____

b How many pounds are equivalent to €475?

_____

_____

_____

c How many pounds are equivalent to €1?

_____

_____

_____

4 Geometry and measures

4.1 3D shapes and surface area

1 The diagram shows a square-based pyramid.
Work out the total surface area of the pyramid.

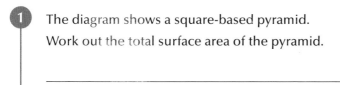

_____

_____

_____

_____

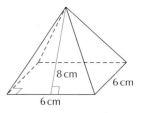

2 Work out the surface area of this sphere.
Give your answer to 3 significant figures.

> **Hint:** Surface area of sphere = $4\pi r^2$,
> where r is the radius.

_____

_____

_____

3 A steel water trough has semi-circular ends, as shown.

The width of the top of the trough is 80 cm.
The length of the trough is 250 cm.

Work out the total surface area of the outside of the water trough.

Give your answer in square metres, to 2 decimal places.

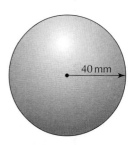

> **Hint:** Surface area of cylinder = $2\pi rh + 2\pi r^2$, where h is the height.

_____

_____

_____

_____

_____

4 A statue is made from a solid cone and a solid cylinder.

A one-litre tin of paint covers 14 m².

Show that the minimum number of tins of paint needed to paint the statue is 6.

Do not include the base of the statue.

> **Hint:** Area of curved surface of cone = $\pi r l$, where l is the slant height.

_____

_____

_____

_____

_____

5 A sphere fits exactly inside a cube.

The surface area of the sphere is 36π cm².

Calculate the total surface area of the cube.

_____

_____

_____

_____

_____

6 **a** A square-based pyramid has a base length of 230 m. The height of the pyramid is 206 m. Use Pythagoras' theorem to find the perpendicular height of one triangular face. Give your answer to 2 decimal places.

_____

_____

_____

b Work out the total surface area of the four triangular faces. Give your answer to 3 significant figures.

_____

_____

_____

4.2 3D shapes – volume

1 **a** Calculate the volume of this cone.

Give your answer to 2 decimal places.

> Hint: Volume of cone $= \frac{1}{3}\pi r^2 h$

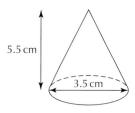

5.5 cm

3.5 cm

_____

_____

_____

b Calculate the volume of this sphere.

Give your answer to 2 decimal places.

> Hint: Volume of sphere $= \frac{4}{3}\pi r^3$

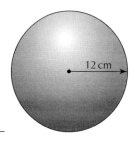

12 cm

_____

_____

_____

2 What is the difference in the volumes of this cuboid and this cone?

> Hint: Volume of cone $= \frac{1}{3}\pi r^2 h$

> Hint: Use consistent units.

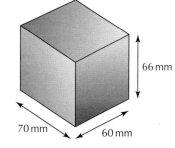

66 mm

70 mm   60 mm

6.2 cm

6.9 cm

Give your answer in cubic centimetres (cm³), to 2 decimal places.

_____

_____

_____

_____

_____

3 **a** A spherical ball is placed in a cylindrical cup full of water.

Find the amount of water displaced by the ball.

Give your answer in millilitres (ml), to 3 significant figures.

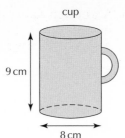

cup   steel ball

9 cm

2cm

8 cm

> Hint: Volume of sphere = $\frac{4}{3}\pi r^3$

> Hint: 1 cm³ holds 1 ml of water.

_____

_____

_____

b Using your answer from part **a**, find the amount of water left in the cup.

Give your answer in ml, to 3 significant figures.

_____

_____

_____

4 A model is made from a hemisphere and a cylinder.

Andrea uses this calculation to find the total volume:

$$\pi \times 10^3 \times 30 + 0.25 \times \frac{4}{3} \times \pi \times 10^2$$

Circle the errors in the calculation.

5 Show that the cone and the cylinder have the same volume.

Give your answers in terms of π.

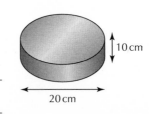

10 cm

20 cm

30 cm

20 cm

_____

_____

_____

_____

6

a A wooden right-angled triangular prism has height 30 cm, width 20 cm and length 60 cm.
A section of the prism with half its height is removed to create a flower box.

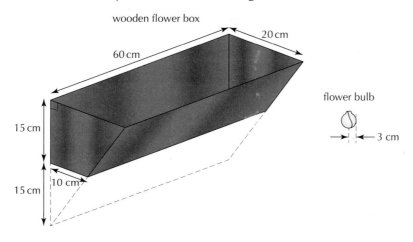

wooden flower box

60 cm

20 cm

15 cm

15 cm

10 cm

flower bulb

3 cm

a Work out the volume of the flower box.

_____

_____

_____

_____

Three spherical bulbs of radius 3 cm are placed in the box.

b Work out the maximum volume of soil that can be placed in the box. Give your answer to 3 significant figures.

Hint: Volume of sphere $= \frac{4}{3}\pi r^3$

_____

_____

_____

4.3 Similarity

 1 *ABC* and *DEF* are similar triangles.

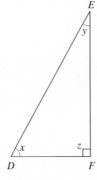

Write the sizes of angles *x*, *y* and *z*, in degrees.

_____

_____

_____

 2 *ABC* and *EFG* are similar triangles.
Work out the length of *FG*.

_____

_____

_____

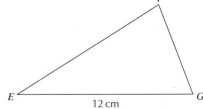

_____

_____

3 In the diagram, *DEF* and *DHG* are straight lines.
EH is parallel to *FG*.
DH is 4 cm, *DG* is 6 cm, *FG* is 10.5 cm.
Sanjit uses this calculation to find the length of *EH*.

$$\frac{6}{4} \times 10.5$$

Give a reason why the calculation is incorrect.

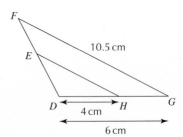

_____

_____

_____

_____

4 ABCD and EFGH are similar trapeziums.

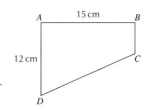

a Show that the length of BC is 4.5 cm.

_____

_____

_____

_____

_____

_____

b Work out the area of trapezium ABCD.

_____

_____

_____

_____

_____

5 In the diagram, prism A and prism B are similar.

a Work out the height of prism A.

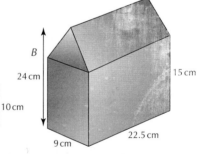

_____

_____

_____

_____

_____

_____

b Work out the difference between the volume of prism A and the volume of prism B.

_____

_____

_____

_____

_____

_____

6 Two cubes A and B have side lengths 5 cm and 2 cm.

Pierre says, 'The ratio of the surface area of cube A to the surface area of cube B is 10:4.'

Is Pierre correct? Give reasons for your answer.

_____

_____

_____

_____

7 Triangles A and B are similar.

The ratio of the area of A to the area of B is 3:5

Read each statement below and decide whether it is true (T) or false (F).

If the statement is false, correct it.

a If the area of A is 3.6 cm², then the area of B is 6 cm²

b If the area of B is 15 cm², then the area of A is 25 cm²

c The area of A is $\frac{3}{5}$ of the area of B.

d The area of B is $\frac{5}{8}$ of the area of A.

_____

_____

_____

_____

_____

_____

8 Two gardens C and D are mathematically similar.

The area of garden C is 450 m².

The area of garden D is 200 m².

The length of one edge of garden C is 7.5 m.

Find the length of the corresponding edge of garden D.

_____

_____

_____

_____

_____

4.4 Trigonometry 🖩

1 *ABC* is a right-angled triangle.

Work out the length of *BC*.
Give your answer to 1 decimal place.

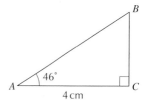

_____

_____

_____

2 *EFG* is a right-angled triangle.

Work out the length of *EG*.
Give your answer to 1 decimal place.

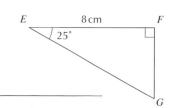

_____

_____

_____

3 *ABC* is a right-angled triangle.

BC = 7.7 cm, angle *ABC* = 35°.

Bert thinks that the calculation to work out the
length of *AC* is 7.7 × 35.

He is not correct.

Write the correct calculation.

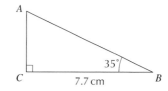

_____

_____

4 *EFGH* is a rectangle.

FG = 2 m, angle *FEG* = 68°.

Show that the length of the diagonal is 2.2 m,
to 1 decimal place.

_____

_____

_____

_____

_____

5 The diagram shows a quadrilateral *RSTV*.

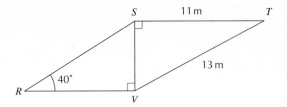

ST = 11 m, *TV* = 13 m, angle *SRV* = 40°.

a Use Pythagoras' theorem to work out the length of *SV*. Give your answer to 3 significant figures.

_____

_____

_____

b Work out the length of *RV*. Give your answer to 3 significant figures.

_____

_____

_____

6 Ali leaves town *C* and walks on a bearing of 335° for 10 km.

How far west from town *C* is he?

Give your answer to 1 decimal place.

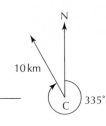

_____

_____

_____

_____

7 *ABCD* is a kite.

BC = 64 mm, angle *ABC* = 60°, angle *BCD* = 130°.

Show that the length of the longest diagonal is 143 mm, to 3 significant figures.

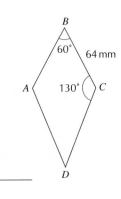

> **Hint:** Divide the kite into two triangles.
> Find the height of each triangle.

_____

_____

_____

_____

4.5 Arcs and sectors 🖩

1 **a** *ABC* is a sector of a circle with radius 4 cm.

Angle *BAC* = 45°.

Work out the length of the arc. Give your answer to 1 decimal place.

_____

_____

_____

_____

b Write the length of the perimeter of the sector. Give your answer to 1 decimal place.

_____

_____

_____

2 *EFG* is a sector of a circle with radius 5 cm.

Angle *BAC* = 60°.

Work out area of the sector. Give your answer to 1 decimal place.

_____

_____

_____

_____

3 **a** The diagram shows a rectangular garden.

The garden is made up from a flower bed and a pond.

One edge of the pond is an arc of a circle.

Work out the area of the flower bed.
Give your answer to 3 significant figures.

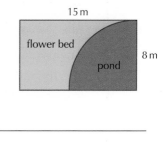

_____

_____

_____

_____

b Work out the area of the pond as a percentage of the area of the garden.
Give your answer to 1 decimal place.

_____

_____

_____

④ *EFG* is a sector of a circle with radius 30 mm.

Angle *FEG* is 60°.

EHJ is an equilateral triangle with side length 20 mm.

Ali writes this calculation for the perimeter of the shape *HFGJ*:

$$20 + 30 + 30 + \frac{60}{360} \times \pi \times 30^2$$

Identify his mistakes.

Write the correct calculation.

_____

_____

_____

_____

_____

⑤ The area of a circle 49π cm².

The area of a sector is $\frac{1}{10}$ the area of a circle.

Show that the length of the perimeter of the sector is 18.4 cm.

⑥ *ACB* is a sector of a circle of radius 20 cm.

BDE is a sector of radius 10 cm.

Angle *ABC* is 120°.

D is the midpoint of *AB*.

E is the midpoint of *AC*.

Show that the area of shape *ADEC* is 100π cm².

_____

_____

_____

_____

_____

4.6 Pythagoras' theorem 🖩

1   *ABC* is a right-angled triangle.

$AC = 12$ cm, $BC = 10$ cm.

Work out the length of *AB*.
Give your answer to 3 significant figures.

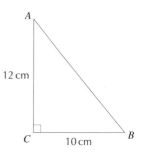

_____

_____

_____

_____

2   *EFG* is a right-angled triangle.

$EF = 13$ cm, $FG = 12$ cm.

Helen uses this method to find the length of *EG*:

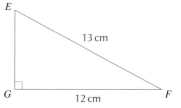

$EG^2 = 13^2 + 12^2$

$EG^2 = 169 + 144$

$EG^2 = 313$

$EG = \sqrt{313}$

$EG = 17.69\ldots$ cm

Is the method correct?

Give reasons for your answer.

_____

_____

_____

_____

_____

3   **a**   The diagram shows a rectangular metal frame
made from 5 rods.

Show that the total length of the 5 rods is 9.5 m.

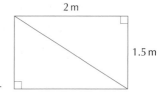

_____

_____

_____

_____

_____

b Work out the length of the diagonal rod as a percentage of the total length of the 5 rods. Give your answer to 1 decimal place.

_____

_____

_____

4 ABCE is a trapezium.
AB = 9 cm, BC = 7 cm, CE = 15 cm

The ratio of length *ED* : length *DC* is 4 : 1.

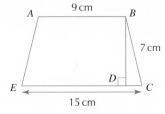

a Work out the perpendicular height of the trapezium. Give your answer to 3 significant figures.

_____

_____

_____

_____

b Work out the area of the trapezium.

_____

Hint: Area of trapezium $= \dfrac{(a+b)}{2}h$

_____

_____

_____

5 ABCD is a kite.

AC = 6 cm (*AE* and *EC* = 3 cm each), BD = 20.4 cm

The ratio of *BE* : *ED* is 5 : 1.

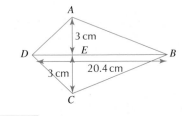

a Work out the length of *ED*.

_____

_____

_____

b Calculate the perimeter of the kite. Give your answer to 3 significant figures.

_____

_____

_____

_____

6 A right-angled triangle has an area of 121 cm².

The sides forming the right angle are in the ratio 2:1

Show that the length of the hypotenuse is $\sqrt{605}$ cm.

_____

_____

_____

_____

7 A triangular prism has base 16 cm, length 25.4 cm and volume of 3048 cm³.

Calculate the surface area of the prism.

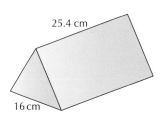

_____

_____

_____

_____

_____

4.7 Congruent triangles

1 The diagram shows triangle *ABC* and triangle *EFG*.

Give the reason why triangle *ABC* and triangle *EFG* are congruent.

_____

_____

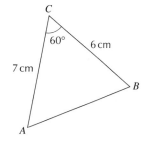
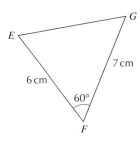

_____

2 The diagram shows triangle *GHJ* and triangle *KLM*.

Explain, giving reasons, why triangle *GHJ* and triangle *KLM* are not congruent.

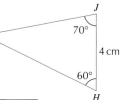
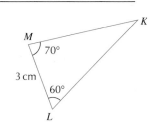

_____

_____

_____

_____

3 EFGH is a parallelogram.

Matt says, 'Triangles EFG and GHE are congruent.'

Is he correct?

Give reasons for your answer.

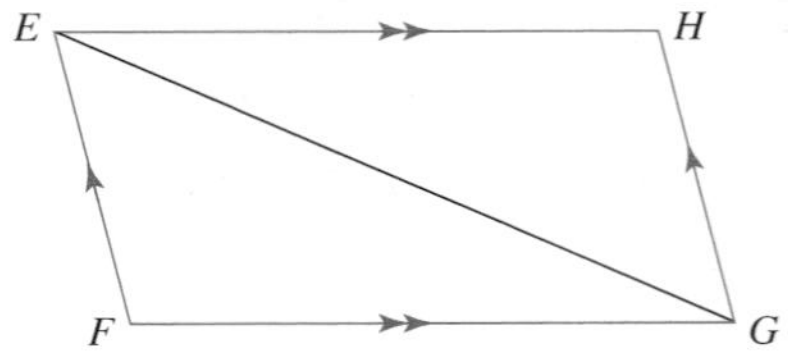

_____

_____

_____

_____

4 In the diagram EJG and HJF are straight lines.

EF and HG are parallel.

Explain why triangle EJH and triangle GJF might not be congruent.

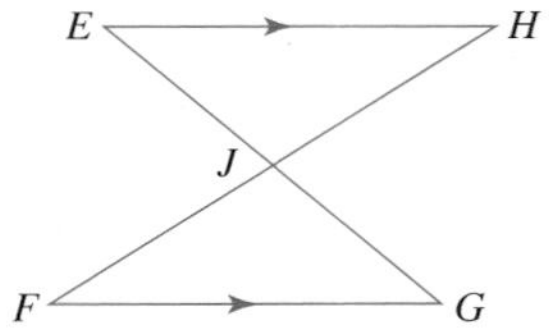

_____

_____

_____

_____

5 **a** ABCDEF is a regular hexagon.

Explain why triangle ABC and triangle CDE are congruent.

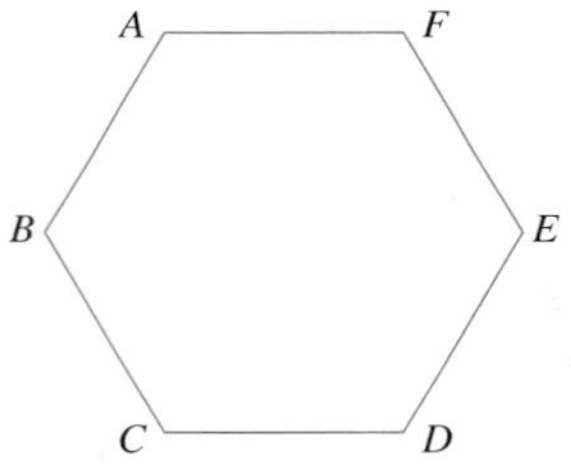

_____

_____

_____

_____

b Write the total number of pairs of congruent triangles in which the triangles are the same size as triangle ABC.

_____

_____

6 *ABCDEFG* is a regular octagon.

AOB is an isosceles triangle.

Show that the area of the octagon is 102 cm²
to 3 significant figures.

> **Hint:** Area of a triangle $= \frac{1}{2}ab\sin C$

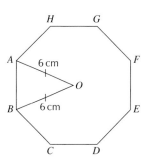

_____

_____

_____

_____

_____

4.8 Regular polygons

1 *ABCDE* is a regular pentagon.

Work out the size of an exterior angle of the pentagon.

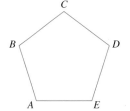

_____

_____

_____

_____

_____

2 *ABCDEFGH* is a regular octagon.

a Work out the size of interior angle *HAB*.

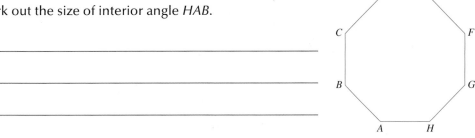

_____

_____

_____

_____

b Work out the sum of the interior angles of the octagon.

_____

_____

_____

_____

3 **a** A regular polygon has 15 sides.

Work out the size of each exterior angle of the polygon.

_____

_____

_____

_____

b Work out the value of the interior angles of the polygon.

_____

_____

_____

4 **a** The interior angles of a regular polygon are 150°.

San uses this method to work out the number of sides.

Exterior angle = 180° − 150°   _____

= 30°   _____

Number of sides = 180° ÷ 30°   _____

= 6   _____

Identify and correct his mistake.

b Work out the sum of the interior angles of the polygon.

_____

_____

_____

5 The diagram shows the interior and exterior angles of a regular polygon.

Show that the polygon has 36 sides.

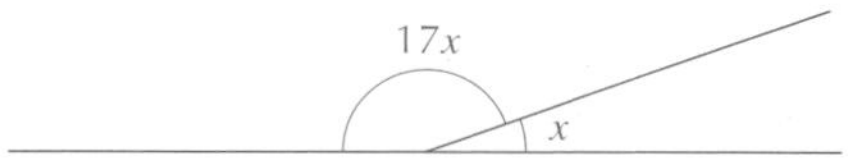

_____

_____

_____

_____

6 **a** The sum of the interior angles of a regular polygon is 1260°.

Find the number of sides of the polygon.

> **Hint:** If a polygon has n sides it can be divided into $(n-2)$ triangles, so $(n-2) \times 180° = 1260°$.

_____

_____

_____

_____

_____

b Calculate the size of an interior angle of the polygon.

_____

_____

_____

4.9 Circle theorems

1 In the diagram, O is the centre of the circle.

AB is a diameter of the circle.

Write the value of p.

Give a reason for your answer.

_____

_____

_____

_____

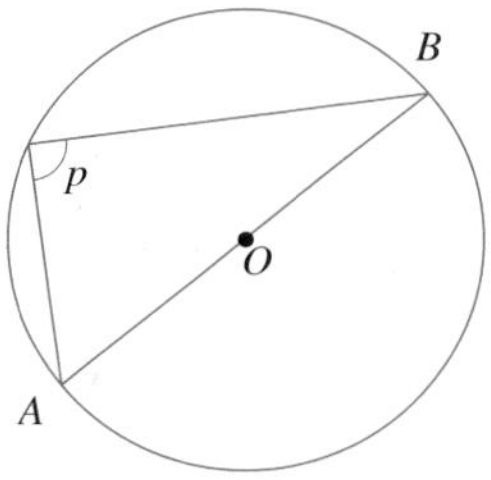

2 In the diagram, O is the centre of the circle.

EF is a diameter of the circle.

Work out the value of r.

Give a reason for your answer.

_____

_____

_____

_____

_____

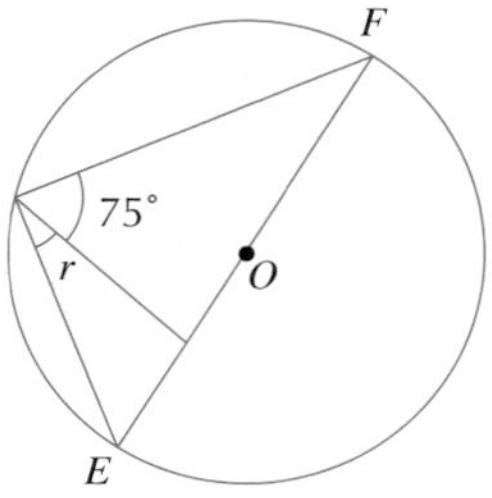

3 In the diagram, O is the centre of the circle.

CD is a diameter of the circle.

EF is a tangent to the circle.

Write the value of s.

Give a reason for your answer.

_____

_____

_____

_____

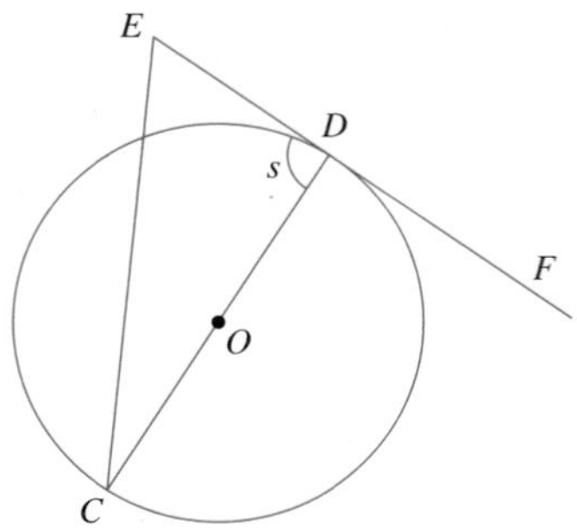

4 Work out the value of a.

Give a reason for your answer.

_____

_____

_____

_____

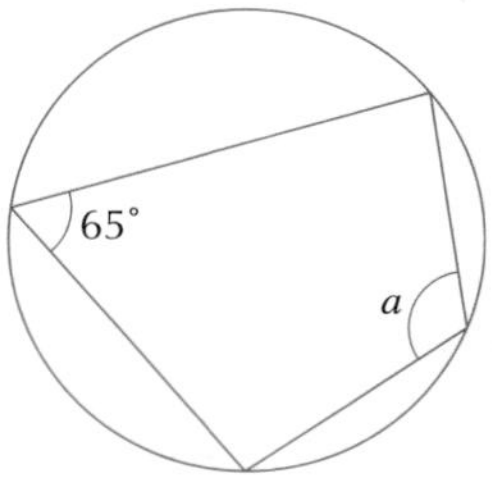

5 Work out the value of b.

Give a reason for your answer.

_____

_____

_____

_____

_____

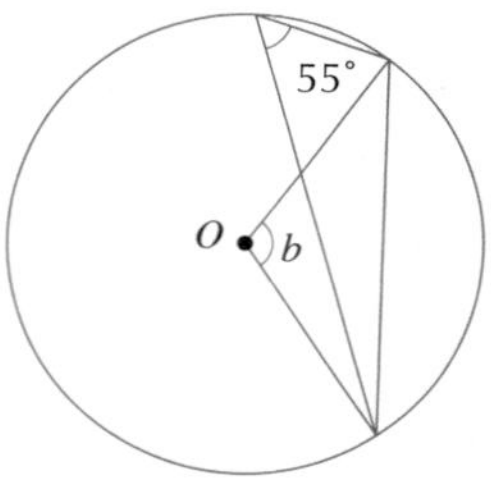

6 In the diagram, O is the centre of the circle.

Work out the value of y.

Give reasons for your answers.

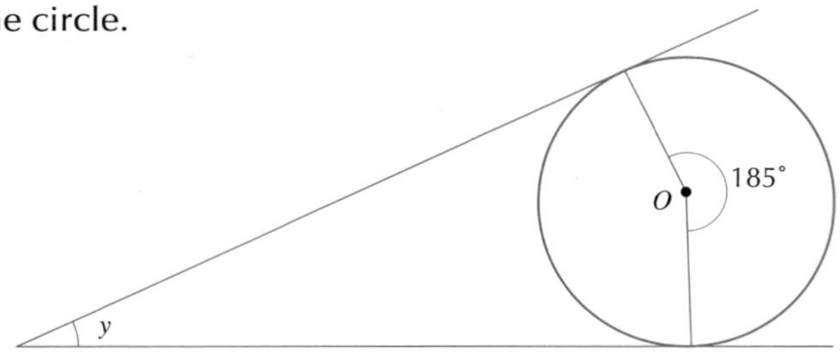

_____

_____

_____

_____

4.10 Translations and vectors

1   **a**   Write the column vector for the translation that maps shape *A* to shape *B*.

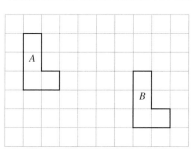

_____

     b   Write the column vector for the translation that maps *C* to *D*.

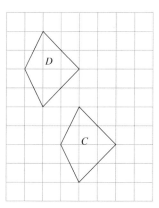

_____

2 $\mathbf{s} = \begin{pmatrix} -3 \\ -1 \end{pmatrix}$, $\mathbf{t} = \begin{pmatrix} 5 \\ 4 \end{pmatrix}$, $\mathbf{v} = \begin{pmatrix} 2 \\ -6 \end{pmatrix}$

     a   On the grid, draw diagrams to represent the column vectors **s**, **t** and **v**.

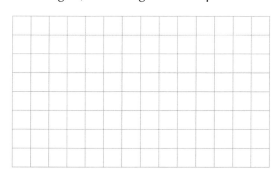

     b   Show that $\mathbf{s} - 2\mathbf{v} = \begin{pmatrix} -7 \\ 11 \end{pmatrix}$.

_____

_____

_____

_____

3 **a** The diagram shows parallelogram $OABC$.

$\vec{OC} = \mathbf{p}$ and $\vec{OA} = \mathbf{q}$.

Write the vector $\vec{AC}$ in terms of $\mathbf{p}$ and $\mathbf{q}$.

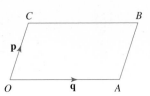

_____

_____

b Write the vector $\vec{OB}$ in terms of $\mathbf{p}$ and $\mathbf{q}$.

_____

4 **a** The diagram shows trapezium $OSTV$.

$\vec{OS} = \mathbf{a}$ and $\vec{OV} = \mathbf{b}$. $ST = 2OV$

Write the vector $\vec{OT}$ in terms of $\mathbf{a}$ and $\mathbf{b}$.

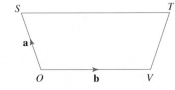

_____

_____

b Write the vector $\vec{VT}$ in terms of $\mathbf{a}$ and $\mathbf{b}$.

_____

_____

5 **a** In the diagram, $\vec{OA} = \mathbf{a}$ and $\vec{OB} = \mathbf{b}$.

M is the midpoint of AB.

Write the vector $\vec{AB}$ in terms of $\mathbf{a}$ and $\mathbf{b}$.

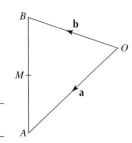

_____

_____

b Write the vector $\vec{AM}$ in terms of $\mathbf{a}$ and $\mathbf{b}$.

_____

_____

c Write the vector $\vec{OM}$ in terms of $\mathbf{a}$ and $\mathbf{b}$.

_____

_____

6 **a** $\mathbf{p} = \begin{pmatrix} a \\ b \end{pmatrix}$, $\mathbf{q} = \begin{pmatrix} 2b \\ a \end{pmatrix}$ and $\mathbf{q} - \mathbf{p} = \begin{pmatrix} 3 \\ 1 \end{pmatrix}$

Show that $a = 5$ and $b = 4$.

_____

_____

_____

_____

_____

b Write the column vectors for **p** and **q**.

_____

4.11 Rotations

1 **a** On the grid, draw the image of triangle *ABC* after a rotation of 90° anticlockwise about the point (−1, 1).

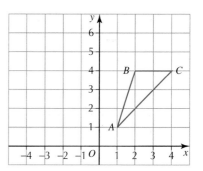

b On the grid, draw the image of parallelogram *CDEF* after a rotation of 180° about the point (−1, −1).

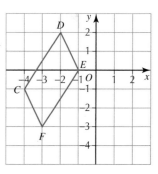

2 **a** The diagram shows shape *A* mapped to shape *B*.

Circle the errors in the description of the transformation:

Rotation, 90° anticlockwise, centre of rotation (−1, 0)

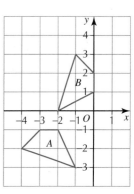

b Describe the **single** transformation that maps shape C to shape D.

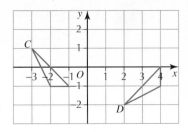

_____

_____

_____

3 The diagram shows shape P on a grid.

The shape is rotated 90° anticlockwise about the point (1, −1).

Write the coordinates of the vertices of the image of P after the rotation.

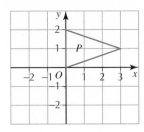

_____

_____

4 **a** The diagram shows trapezium A on a grid.

Trapezium A is rotated 90° clockwise about the point (1, 3), to give trapezium B.

Trapezium B is then rotated 90° anticlockwise about the point (1, −1) to give trapezium C.

On the grid, draw trapezium C.

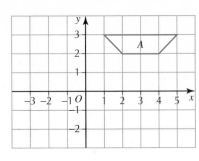

b Write the **single** transformation that maps trapezium A to trapezium C.

_____

_____

5 **a** The diagram shows kite P on a grid.

The kite is rotated 90° clockwise about the point (−1, 1) to give kite Q.

Kite Q is then rotated 180° about the point (0, 0) to give kite R.

Write the coordinates of the vertices of kite R.

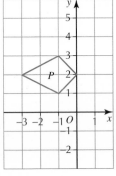

_____

_____

b Kite P is now rotated 180° about the point (0, 0) to give kite S.

Kite S is rotated 90° clockwise about the point (−1, 1) to give kite T.

Sam says, 'Kite T will be in the same position as kite R.'

Is she correct?

You must show your working.

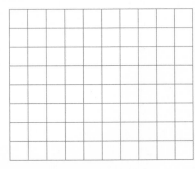

6 A polygon plotted on a grid has a vertex at (x, y).

The polygon is rotated 180° about (0, 0).

Write the new position of the vertex.

_____

4.12 Reflections

1 **a** On this grid, draw the image of quadrilateral ABCD after a reflection in the line $x = 0$.

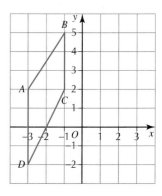

b On this grid, draw the image of triangle ABC after a reflection in the line $y = x$.

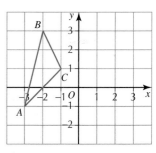

2 **a** The diagram shows triangle A and triangle B drawn on a grid.

Describe the **single** transformation that maps triangle A to triangle B.

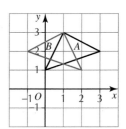

_____

_____

_____

b The diagram shows shape C and shape D drawn on a grid.

Circle and correct the error in the description of the transformation of shape C to shape D.

Reflection, line $y = x$ _____

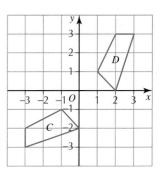

3 The diagram shows triangle A drawn on a grid.

Triangle A is reflected in the line $x = 1$ to give triangle B.

Triangle B is then reflected in the line $y = -x$ to give triangle C.

On the grid, draw triangle C.

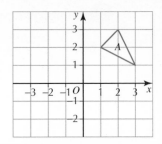

4 On the grid, shape R is transformed by two reflections to create image S.

Write the equations of the two lines of reflection.

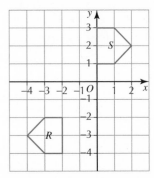

5 On the grid, triangle F is reflected in the line $y = x$ to give triangle G. Triangle G is reflected in the line $y = 0$ to give triangle H.

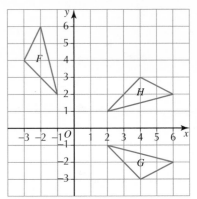

Pete says, 'If triangle F is reflected in the line $x = 0$ and this image is reflected in the line $y = x$, the new image will be in the same position as triangle H.'

Is he correct?

Show your working on the grid on the right.

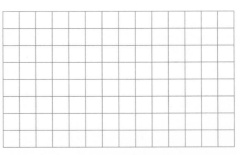

6 **a** The diagram shows parallelogram P drawn on a grid.

Parallelogram P is reflected in the line $y = 2.5$ to give parallelogram Q.

Parallelogram Q is then reflected in the line $y = -x$ to give parallelogram R.

On the grid, draw parallelogram R.

b Write the **single** transformation that maps parallelogram P to parallelogram R.

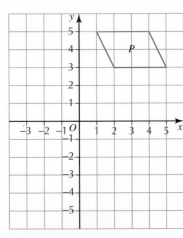

_____

_____

4.13 Enlargements

1 On the grid, draw the image of pentagon *ABCDE* after an enlargement by scale factor 3, centre (−3, −2).

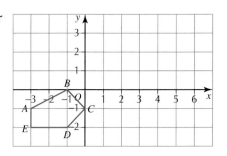

2 On the grid, draw the image of triangle *EFG* after an enlargement by scale factor 2, centre (6, 4).

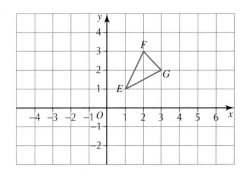

3 The diagram shows shape *A* and shape *B*.

Rita says that shape *B* is an enlargement of shape *A*.

Explain why Rita is wrong.

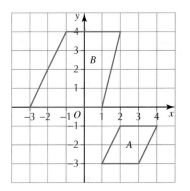

_____

_____

_____

_____

4 The diagram shows shape *C* and shape *D*.

Describe **fully** the transformation that maps shape *C* to shape *D*.

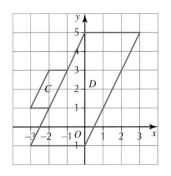

_____

_____

_____

_____

5 On the grid, draw the image of triangle *RST* after an enlargement by scale factor $\frac{1}{2}$, centre (−8, −2).

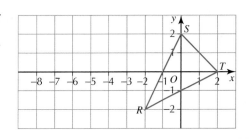

6 **a** The diagram shows shape *A* mapped to shape *B*.

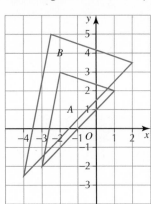

Show that the centre of enlargement is (−1, −1).

_____

_____

_____

_____

_____

_____

b Work out the scale factor of enlargement.

_____

_____

_____

c Write the scale factor of enlargement that maps shape *B* to shape *A*.

_____

_____

_____

7 On the grid, draw the image of parallelogram *RSTV* after an enlargement by scale factor $\frac{3}{4}$, centre (2, 1).

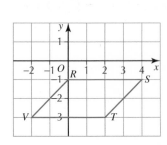

4.14 Constructions

1 **a** Using a pair of compasses and a ruler, construct the perpendicular bisector of line segment *AB*.

A ———————————— B

b Using a pair of compasses and a ruler, construct the perpendicular to line *CD* from point *P*.

2 Using a pair of compasses and a ruler, construct the angle bisector of angle *AOB*.

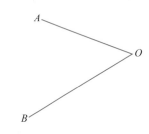

3 **a** Using a pair of compasses and a ruler, construct the angle bisector of angle *PRS*.

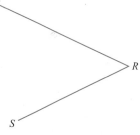

b Mark point *B* on the bisector, 35 mm from *R*.

Using a pair of compasses and a ruler, construct the shortest distance from *B* to line *PR*.

4 **a** Using a pair of compasses and a ruler, construct a triangle *ABC* with:

$AB = 40\,mm$, $BC = 60\,mm$, $AC = 80\,mm$

b Using a pair of compasses and a ruler, construct the angle bisector of *BAC* so that it cuts *BC* at *P*.

c Write the ratio of *BP* : *PC*. _____

5　**a** Using a pair of compasses and a ruler, construct triangle *ABC* with:

　　$AB = 50\,\text{mm}$, $BC = 45\,\text{mm}$, $AC = 35\,\text{mm}$

　b Using a pair of compasses and a ruler, find the point of intersection of all the angle bisectors of the interior angles of your triangle.

6　Using a pair of compasses and a ruler, construct a diameter of a circle that is perpendicular to a chord that it bisects.

4.15 Loci ✖

1 Construct the locus of points that are 25 mm from line segment *AB*.

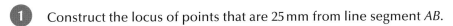

A ———————— B

2 *PQRS* is a rectangle.

P ———————— Q

S ———————— R

a Construct the locus of points inside the rectangle that are equidistant from *PS* and *QR*.

b Construct the locus of points inside the rectangle that are equidistant from *PQ* and *PS*.

c Belle says that there is no region that is closer to *QR* than *PS* **and** closer to *PS* than *PQ*. Using shading, show that she is incorrect.

3 Here is triangle *PRS*.

Construct the locus of points that are 1 cm from the outside edge of the triangle.

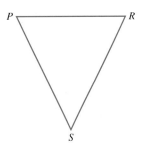

4 *TVWXYZ* is a hexagon.

Shade the region inside the hexagon where the points are:

i nearer to *TV* than *TZ*,

ii nearer to *TZ* than *VW*

iii less than 25 mm from *X*.

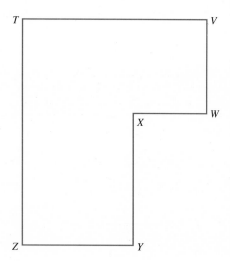

5 **a** Using a pair of compasses and a ruler, construct an equilateral triangle with side length 50 mm.

b On your triangle, construct the locus of points within the triangle that are 25 mm from a vertex.

c Show that the area within the triangle for all points more than 25 mm from each vertex is 101 mm^2 to 3 significant figures.

Hint: Area of triangle $= \frac{1}{2} ab \sin C$.

_____

_____

_____

_____

_____

6 **a** Using a pair of compasses and a ruler, construct triangle ABC with:

$AB = 32$ mm, $BC = 30$ mm, $CA = 18$ mm.

b Point P is equidistant from AB and BC.

P is also 45 mm from C.

Mark the two possible positions of P on your diagram.

5 Probability

5.1 Basic probability

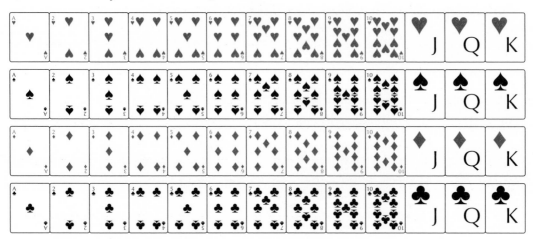

1 A card is selected from a pack of cards.

a What is the probability of selecting a black Jack?

_____

b What is the probability of selecting a picture card or a 10?

_____

c What is the probability of not selecting an 8 or a 9?

_____

_____

d Show that the probability of selecting an even number is **not** the same as the probability of selecting a prime number.

_____

_____

_____

_____

2 Anton throws a dice 120 times.

The results are shown in the table.

Number on dice	1	2	3	4	5	6
Frequency	12	21	24	27	11	25
Relative frequency						

a Work out the relative frequency for each number on the dice.

_____

_____

_____

b If the dice is fair, how many times would you expect it to land on each number?

_____

c Do you think the dice is fair? Give a reason for your answer.

_____

_____

_____

3 In a game, players choose a number from 1 to 60, at random.

They play 300 games.

The number 54 is chosen more than any other number.

Dan says, '54 is the most likely number to be chosen.'

Is he correct?

Give a reason for your answer.

_____

_____

_____

_____

4 In a game, a letter of the alphabet is chosen at random.

520 games are played.

The letter G is selected the fewest times.

Is the game biased?

Give a reason your answer.

_____

_____

_____

_____

5.2 Sample spaces and experimental probability 🖩

1 A bag contains 100 beads.
All the beads are either blue or red.

A bead is taken from the bag at random,
its colour is noted and the bead is replaced.

This is done 1000 times.

The table shows the numbers of blue beads
selected after 10, 50, 100, 500 and 1000 trials.

Number of trials	Number of blue beads selected
10	4
50	24
100	52
500	280
1000	598

a Work out the experimental probability for
each trial.

_____

_____

_____

_____

_____

b Use the results of the experiment to estimate the number of red balls in the bag.
You must show your working.

_____

_____

_____

_____

2 Ann has two spinners.

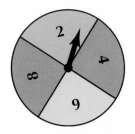 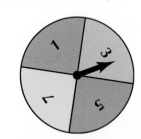

She spins both spinners and
adds together the scores
where the arrows stop.
The sample space diagram
shows the totals.

		Spinner 1			
	+	2	4	6	8
	1	3	5	7	9
Spinner 2	3	5	7	9	11
	5	7	9	11	13
	7	9	11	13	15

Ann says that the spinners are not fair because the total of 9 appears more than any other number in the sample space diagram.

Is she correct?

Explain your answer.

_____

_____

_____

_____

_____

_____

3 Tom throws two dice and multiplies the scores together to give the result.

The sample space diagram shows all the possible outcomes.

		Dice 1					
		1	**2**	**3**	**4**	**5**	**6**
	1	1	2	3	4	5	6
	2	2	4	6	8	10	12
Dice 2	**3**	3	6	9	12	15	18
	4	4	8	12	16	20	24
	5	5	10	15	20	25	30
	6	6	12	18	24	30	36

a Assuming that the dice are fair, explain why the probability of getting an odd result is much less than that of getting an even result.

_____

_____

_____

_____

b In fact, one of the dice is biased and is less likely to land on the number 6.

How will this affect the probability of an even total?

_____

_____

4 Mia throws a fair coin three times and records the outcomes.

First throw	Second throw	Third throw	Outcome
H	H	H	HHH
		T	HHT
	T	H	HTH
		T	HTT
T	H	H	THH
		T	THT
	T	H	TTH
		T	TTT

a Using the sample space diagram, show that the probability of getting exactly two heads is $\frac{3}{8}$.

_____

_____

_____

_____

b Given that the first throw gives heads (H) and the second throw gives heads (H), what is the probability that the outcome of the three throws will be HHH?

Hint: The answer is **not** $\frac{1}{8}$.

_____

_____

c Mia throws the three coins 160 times.

How many times should she expect to get HHH?

_____

5.3 The probability of combined events

1 A biased coin is thrown twice. The probability of throwing a head is $\frac{5}{8}$ and the

probability of throwing a tail is $\frac{3}{8}$.

Hint: Two events are said to be **independent** if the outcome of one event does not affect the outcome of the other event.

Hint: The probability of **two independent outcomes**, A and B, **both** happening is given by:
$$P(A \text{ and } B) = P(A) \times P(B)$$

What is the probability of throwing:

a two tails _____

_____

b two heads _____

_____

c a head followed by a tail? _____

_____

2 An ordinary fair dice is rolled twice.

Show that the probability of rolling a prime number followed by a 4 is $\frac{1}{12}$.

_____

_____

_____

_____

3 A bag contains 3 red beads and 4 black beads.

A bead is chosen at random from the bag.
The colour is recorded and the bead is put back in the bag.

Another bead is then chosen at random from the bag.

Alice says that there is a 50% chance of getting a red bead and a black bead, in either order.

Is she correct?

Give a reason for your answer.

_____

_____

_____

_____

4 The probability that Ajay meets his friend on any day is 0.85.

Ajay wants to work out the probability that he does **not** meet his friend on two consecutive days.

This is his working.

$$P(not\ meet) = 1 - 0.85$$
$$= 0.15$$

$P(not\ meet\ and\ not\ meet)$ is $0.15 + 0.15 = 0.3$

Find the mistake in his calculation and correct it.

_____

_____

_____

_____

5 The probability that Sanjay walks to school is 0.7.

The probability that he has a school lunch is 0.4.

a What is the probability that Sanjay:

i walks to school and has a school lunch?

_____

_____

ii does not walk to school and has a school lunch?

_____

_____

iii walks to school and does not have a school lunch?

_____

_____

iv does not walk to school and does not have a school lunch?

_____

_____

b Give a reason why the sum of the four probabilities in part **a** should equal 1.

_____

_____

6 Amy selects a card from an ordinary pack and then replaces it.
She then shuffles the pack and selects another card.
Draw lines to match the events to their probabilities.

a P(an ace and an ace)　　　　　　　　　　　　**i** $\dfrac{3}{169}$

b P(an ace and a picture card)　　　　　　　　**ii** $\dfrac{1}{169}$

c P(a picture card and a picture card)　　　　**iii** $\dfrac{100}{169}$

d P(not a picture card and not a picture card)　**iv** $\dfrac{9}{169}$

7 An ordinary fair dice is rolled three times.
What is the probability of rolling three sixes?

_____

_____

8 The probability of a biased four-sided spinner landing on a 3 twice in a row is 0.16. What is the probability of the spinner **not** landing on a 3?

_____

_____

_____

5.4 Frequency trees 🖩

1 800 students took part in a school sports day.

Before the sports day each student predicted whether or not they would get a medal.

275 students predicted they would get a medal.

170 students who predicted they would get a medal, did so.

300 medals were awarded on sports day.

a Complete the frequency tree for these outcomes.

b Work out the fraction of the 800 students whose predictions were correct.

Give your answer in its simplest form.

_____

_____

_____

_____

Prediction   Actual outcome

medal

medal

no medal

no medal

medal

no medal

c What percentage of the students who did not get a medal predicted that they would get a medal?

_____

_____

2 300 people took a test in two parts.

The probability that a person, chosen at random, passes the first part of the test is 0.75.

The probability that a person, chosen at random, passes the second part of the test is 0.6.

a Complete the frequency tree for these outcomes.

b How many people passed both parts of the test?

_____

_____

_____

_____

First part   Second part

pass

pass

fail

pass

fail

fail

c What percentage of people did not pass both parts of the test?

_____

_____

_____

_____

5.5 Tree diagrams

1 A biased coin is thrown twice.

The probability of scoring a head is $\frac{2}{5}$.

a Complete the probability tree diagram for these outcomes.

b Use the tree diagram to work out the probability of scoring:

   i two heads _____

_____

_____

   ii two tails _____

_____

   iii a head followed by a tail. _____

_____

First throw **Second throw**

head

head

tail

head

tail

tail

2 A bag contains 3 red beads and 5 black beads.

A bead is chosen at random from the bag, its colour is recorded and the bead is replaced in the bag.

Another bead is then chosen from the bag.

a Draw a probability tree diagram for these outcomes.

b Show that the probability of choosing two beads of the same colour is $\frac{17}{32}$.

_____

_____

_____

_____

c Work out the probability that at least one bead is red.

_____

_____

_____

3 A test has two parts.

The probability that a person passes the first part is 0.75.

The probability that a person passes the second part is 0.6.

a Complete the probability tree diagram for these outcomes.

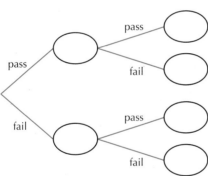

b Work out the probability that a person passes both parts of the test.

_____

_____

c Explain how you can use you answer to part **b**, and your knowledge of the sum of the probabilities for all possible outcomes, to work out the probability that a person does not pass both parts of the test.

_____

_____

4 A card is chosen, at random, from an ordinary pack and then replaced.

The pack is shuffled and another card is chosen, at random, and replaced.

The pack is then shuffled again and a third card is chosen, at random.

> Hint: Look back at the hint at the start of this chapter, if you need to remind yourself of the contents of a pack of cards.

a Complete the probability tree diagram.

First choice   Second choice   Third choice

King   King   King / not King

not King   King / not King

b Find the probability that three Kings are chosen.

_____

_____

c Find the probability that at least two Kings are chosen.

_____

_____

_____

_____

_____

_____

5.6 Venn diagrams

1 The table shows six Venn diagrams. One of the diagrams has no shading.

The set notations for the Venn diagrams are given.

Draw lines to match each completed Venn diagram to its notation.

Then shade the blank Venn diagram to illustrate the unmatched set notation and draw a line between them.

Venn diagram	Notation

a

$A \cup B$

b

$A \cap B$

c

$A \cap B'$

d

A'

e

$(A \cup B)'$

f

$(A \cap B)'$

2 A sixth form has 40 students.

21 of these 40 students study Mathematics.

13 study Mathematics and Biology.

8 students are studying neither Mathematics nor Biology.

a Complete the Venn diagram to show this information.

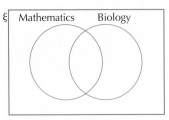

b A student is chosen at random.

   i Work out P(M').

_____

_____

   ii Work out P($M \cup B$)'.

_____

_____

   iii Work out P($M \cap B$).

_____

_____

3 A group of 30 students play musical instruments.

Some play the guitar (G).

Some play the piano (P).

Some play both the guitar and the piano.

Some play neither the guitar nor the piano.

Listed below are some probabilities for a student chosen at random from this group.

P(G) = $\frac{1}{3}$ P(P) = $\frac{3}{5}$ P($G \cup P$)' = $\frac{1}{6}$

a Complete the Venn diagram with the numbers of students.

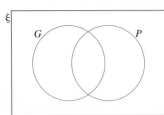

b What fraction of students don't play the guitar and don't play the piano?

_____

_____

6 Statistics

6.1 Pie charts and composite and dual bar charts

1 The pie chart shows the musical instruments played by some students.

11 students play the guitar.

How many students does the pie chart represent?

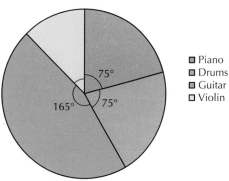

- Piano
- Drums
- Guitar
- Violin

165° 75° 75°

_____

_____

_____

_____

_____

2 The table shows a group of people's favourite political parties.

This data is to be represented in a pie chart.

a Show that each person will be represented by $\frac{2°}{3}$.

Party	Number of people
Conservative	264
Labour	218
SNP	29
LD	10
DUP	8
Other	11

_____

_____

_____

_____

b Show that the Labour sector will be 145° to the nearest degree.

_____

_____

3 The pie charts show the film preferences of a group of girls and a group of boys.

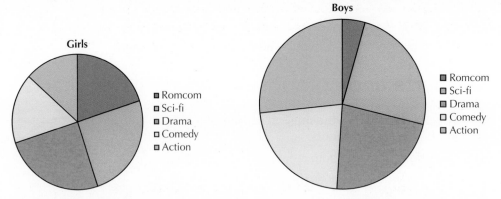

Did the same number of girls and boys prefer sci-fi? You must explain your answer.

_____

_____

_____

4 The dual bar chart shows how the employees of a company usually travel to work.

Show that the number of people who travel by car is not more than the sum of the people who travel by all the other modes of transport.

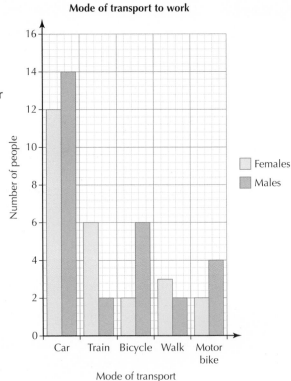

_____

_____

_____

_____

_____

_____

_____

5 The composite bar chart shows Mathematics GCSE results for a group of students.

Evaluate each of the following statements. deciding whether you agree or disagree. Where you disagree, explain why.

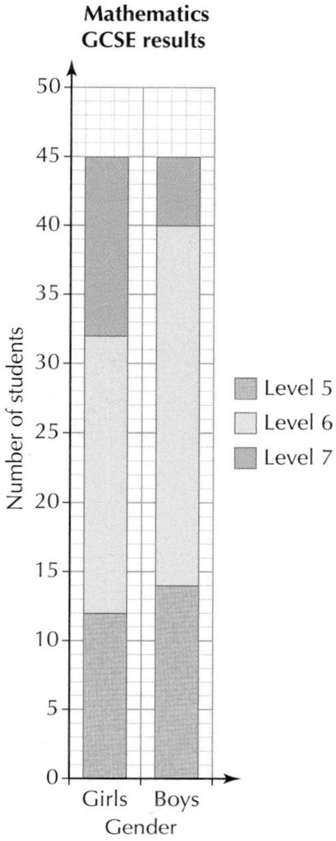

a The bar chart represents different numbers of girls and boys.

_____

_____

_____

b A greater proportion of boys than girls achieved Level 6.

_____

_____

_____

c A greater proportion of boys than girls achieved Level 7.

_____

_____

_____

d A smaller proportion of girls than boys achieved Level 5.

_____

_____

_____

e Most of the boys achieved Level 6.

_____

_____

_____

Mathematics GCSE results

Number of students

Girls Boys
Gender

Level 5
Level 6
Level 7

6.2 Grouped frequency tables 🔲

1 The table shows the times, in minutes, and how often 38 people exercise on one day.

Times, t (minutes)	Frequency
$0 < t \leqslant 10$	2
$10 < t \leqslant 20$	8
$20 < t \leqslant 30$	12
$30 < t \leqslant 40$	5
$40 < t \leqslant 50$	7
$50 < t \leqslant 60$	4

a Estimate the total number of minutes these people spent exercising.

_____

_____

_____

_____

_____

_____

b State why your answer to part **a** is an estimate.

_____

_____

c Work out an estimate of the mean number of minutes of exercise per person.

_____

_____

_____

2 The mean of the following data is 3.3125.

What is the hidden frequency in the table?

_____

_____

You must show your working.

x	Frequency
1	8
2	15
3	13
4	⬛
5	9
6	7

_____

_____

3 The tables summarises the ages of some members of a gym.

Age (years)	Frequency
12–21	9
22–31	16
32–41	15
42–51	12
52–61	5
62–71	3

Kyle says that the range of ages of gym members is 59 years.

Is he correct?

Give a reason for your answer.

_____

_____

_____

4 The table shows the time a person takes to travel to work each day over two months.

Time, t (minutes)	Frequency
20–24	5
25–29	10
30–34	21
35–39	3
40–44	2
45–49	2

Show how to work out from the table which group contains the median.

_____

_____

_____

_____

_____

_____

_____

5 The table shows the heights of 25 sunflowers when fully grown.

Height, h (metres)	Frequency
$0 < h \leqslant 0.5$	a
$0.5 < h \leqslant 1.0$	5
$1.0 < h \leqslant 1.5$	b
$1.5 < h \leqslant 2$	6

a Show that $a + b = 14$.

_____

_____

_____

_____

b The estimated mean height is 1.19 m.

Work out the values of a and b.

You must show your working.

_____

_____

_____

_____

_____

_____

_____

_____

_____

_____

_____

6.3 Correlation

1 The table shows the results of some students in a Mathematics test and a French test.

Student	Mathematics	French
A	92	87
B	86	90
C	81	82
D	75	76
E	56	14
F	52	65
G	41	51
H	66	68
J	60	59
K	58	65

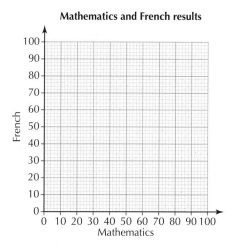

Mathematics and French results

a Plot the results on the scatter diagram provided.

b Describe the type and strength of correlation. Explain why you chose your answer.

_____

_____

_____

_____

c Draw a line of best fit on your scatter diagram, above.

d A student was absent for the French test. Her result on the Mathematics test was 65. Use the scatter graph to estimate her French result.

_____

e Identify any results that are outliers.

_____

_____

2 Describe the type of correlation in each diagram.
Where possible, describe the strength of the correlation.

a **Comparison of lengths**

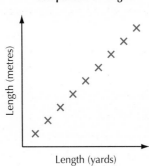

_____

_____

b **Number of siblings
and shoe sizes**

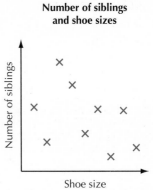

_____

_____

c **Comparison of temperature
and sales of ice cream**

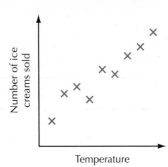

_____

_____

d **Comparison of size of portion
of pizza and the number of
people sharing it**

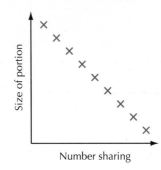

_____

_____

e **Comparison of sales of ice
cream and umbrellas**

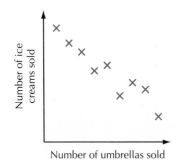

_____

_____

3 Scatter diagrams are plotted for six different pairs of data.

Hint: Correlation does not imply causation.

The table shows the pairs of data and the type of correlation shown on each scatter diagram.

	Variable 1	Variable 2	Correlation
a	English test results	Mathematics test results	Positive
b	Number of flu jabs given	People with flu	Negative
c	Shoe size	English test result	No correlation
d	Mathematics GCSE result	Mathematics A-level result	Positive
e	Biscuit sales	Age of purchaser	No correlation
f	Number of days absent from school	GCSE Mathematics grade	Negative

For each data pair, describe the relationship between the variables based on the correlation.

a _____

b _____

c _____

d _____

e _____

f _____

4 The scatter diagram shows the correlation between two variables, 1 and 2.

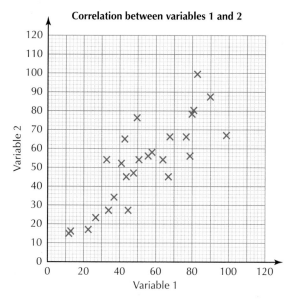

Correlation between variables 1 and 2

Use a line of best fit to estimate the value of variable 1 when variable 2 is 60.

_____

6.4 Time series graphs

1 The table shows the temperatures in a village one July over a 24-hour period.

Time	Temperature (°C)
00:00	18
01:00	18
02:00	18
03:00	18
04:00	18
05:00	18
06:00	18
07:00	19
08:00	20
09:00	20
10:00	21
11:00	21

Time	Temperature (°C)
12:00	22
13:00	23
14:00	23
15:00	24
16:00	25
17:00	24
18:00	24
19:00	23
20:00	21
21:00	20
22:00	19
23:00	18

a Plot a time series graph for this data on the grid provided.

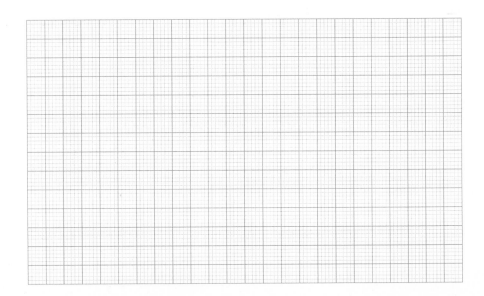

b Use your graph to estimate the temperature at 09:30.

_____

_____

c Describe how the temperature changes over the 24 hours.

_____

_____

2

a Which of the following statements are true for time series graphs? Write T (for 'true') or F (for 'false').

  i A time series graph shows changes over time.

_____

  ii A time series graph can be used to predict trends.

_____

  iii The vertical scale on a time series graph always starts at 0.

_____

  iv A time series graph can be used by joining plotted points with straight lines to read off exact values between the plotted points.

_____

  v A time series graph can be used by joining plotted points with straight lines to read off estimates between the plotted points.

_____

b Give an example of a data set that could be shown on a times series graph. Explain why you think a time series graph would be a good way to display the data set that you have chosen.

_____

_____

_____

_____

3 The time series graph shows the numbers of visitors, to the nearest 10 000, arriving by air in Iceland each year from 2010 to 2016.

a Use your graph to estimate the number of visitors arriving in 2017.

_____

_____

_____

_____

b Between which two years was the greatest increase in visitor numbers? Explain how you know.

_____

_____

_____

_____

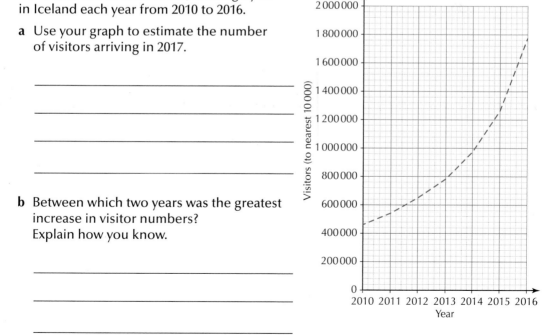

Visitors arriving in Iceland by air

Visitors (to nearest 10 000)

4 The table shows the numbers of GCSE entries over a ten-year period.

Year	Number of GCSE entries (to the nearest 10 000)
2000	5 480 000
2001	5 630 000
2002	5 660 000
2003	5 730 000
2004	5 880 000
2005	5 740 000
2006	5 750 000
2007	5 830 000
2008	5 670 000
2009	5 470 000

The chart shows the numbers of GCSE entries, plotted on a time series graph.

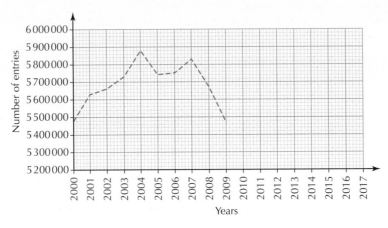

a Identify the four errors or omissions from the graph. Correct the graph.

_____

_____

_____

_____

b Use the graph to describe how GCSE entries changed between 2000 and 2009.

_____

_____

c Compare the change in GCSE entries from 2000 to 2001 with those from 2005 to 2006.

_____

_____

6.5 Cumulative frequency and box plots

1 The table shows the ages of 100 people at a party.

Age, a (completed years)	Frequency	
$0 < a \leqslant 10$	5	
$10 < a \leqslant 20$	8	
$20 < a \leqslant 30$	11	
$30 < a \leqslant 40$	19	
$40 < a \leqslant 50$	26	
$50 < a \leqslant 60$	12	
$60 < a \leqslant 70$	8	
$70 < a \leqslant 80$	8	
$80 < a \leqslant 90$	2	
$90 < a \leqslant 100$	1	

a How many people at the party were aged 20 or under?

_____

_____

b How many people at the party were aged over 70?

_____

_____

c Was there anyone at the party aged over 100? Give a reason for your answer.

_____

_____

d Draw a cumulative frequency graph for this data.

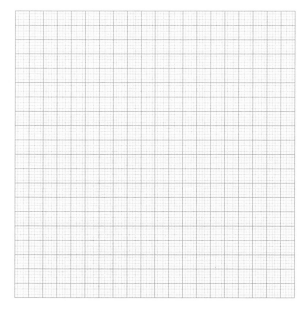

> **Hint:** Cumulative frequency is plotted against the upper class boundary for each class interval.

e Use your graph to estimate:

   i the median of the ages

   _____

   ii the lower quartile of the ages

   _____

   iii the upper quartile of the ages

   _____

   iv the interquartile range of the ages.

   _____

f Explain why all the answers in part **e** are estimates.

_____

_____

2 Monty measured the heights of some plants in his garden.

He drew this cumulative frequency graph for the data.

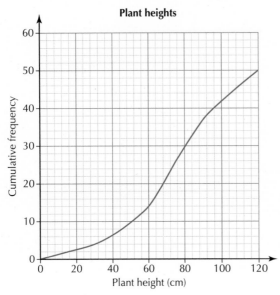

a How many plants were measured?

_____

b Use the cumulative frequency graph to estimate the number of plants with heights between 30 cm and 60 cm.

_____

_____

c What is the probability that one of these plants, chosen at random, has a height between 30 cm and 60 cm?

_____

_____

d A gardener is going to cut down all the plants with heights over 90 cm.

Estimate the percentage of these plants that he is going to cut down.

_____

_____

3 The times that 200 students wait in a lunch queue are recorded.

Here is a cumulative frequency graph for the data.

The shortest waiting time was 5 seconds and the longest waiting time was 59 seconds.

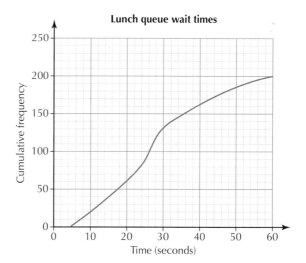

Lunch queue wait times

Duane draws this box plot for the data in the cumulative frequency graph.

Identify the two mistakes on his box plot.

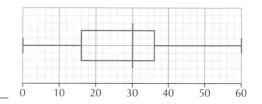

_____

_____

4 A cinema is showing two films, A and B.

The table shows data about the ages of people attending the cinema to watch film A.

	Age (years)
Youngest	5
Lower quartile	11
Median	22
Upper quartile	38
Oldest	91

a Work out the interquartile range of people watching film A.

_____

_____

b Draw a box plot for the data.

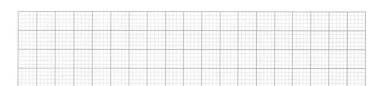

The box plot on the right shows data about the ages of the people attending the cinema to watch film B.

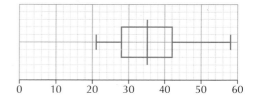

c Compare the ages of people watching film A with the ages of people watching film B.

_____

_____

_____

_____

6.6 Histograms 🖩

1 The table shows the time it takes for some children to walk to school.

Time, *t* (minutes)	Frequency	Class width	Frequency density
$0 < t \leqslant 5$	1		
$5 < t \leqslant 10$	5		
$10 < t \leqslant 15$	2		
$15 < t \leqslant 20$	12		

Hint: Frequency density = $\dfrac{\text{frequency for class interval}}{\text{width of class interval}}$

Hint: Frequency density is plotted on the vertical axis

Draw a histogram for this data.

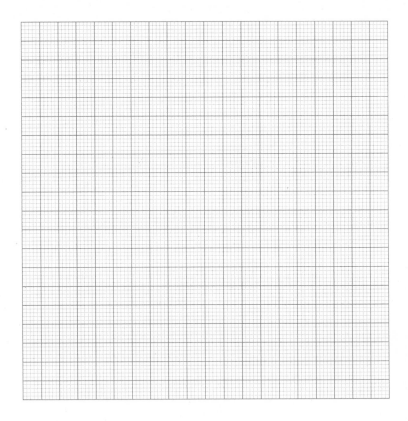

2 The table shows the heights of some Year 11 students.

Height, h (cm)	Frequency	Class width	Frequency density
$160 < h \leqslant 167$	7		
$167 < h \leqslant 170$	12		
$170 < h \leqslant 175$	13		
$175 < h \leqslant 177$	11		
$177 < h \leqslant 180$	6		

a Draw a histogram for this data.

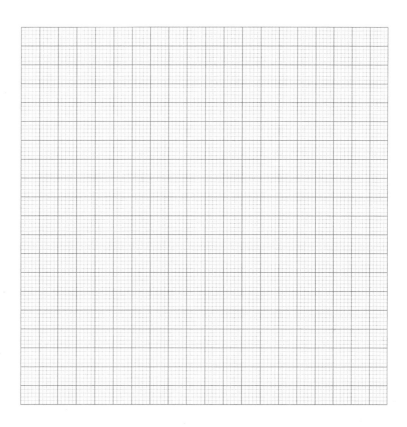

b Use your histogram to work out an estimate for the number of students with height less than 168 cm.

_____

_____

_____

c Use your histogram to work out an estimate for the number of students with height greater than 178 cm.

_____

_____

_____

3 The table shows the results of a survey of the speeds of vehicles as they enter a 30 mph speed limit.

Speed, s (mph)	Frequency	Class width	Frequency density
$0 < s \leqslant 15$	3		
$15 < s \leqslant 20$	4		
$20 < s \leqslant 25$	6		
$25 < s \leqslant 30$	18		
$30 < s \leqslant 40$	7		
$40 < s \leqslant 50$	2		

a Complete the table, then draw a histogram for this data.

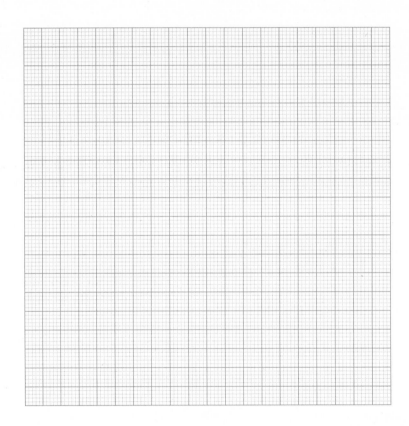

b Work out the total number of vehicles in the survey.

_____

_____

c Estimate the number of vehicles travelling at more than 5 mph above the speed limit.

_____

_____

6.7 Sampling 🖩

1 A school needs to take a sample of 100 students.

For each of the following, decide whether the method of sampling will give a random, unbiased sample. Give a reason for your answer.

a Select the first 100 students who arrive at school in the morning.

_____

_____

_____

_____

b Ask for volunteers from Year 7.

_____

_____

_____

_____

c Make a list of all the students, in alphabetical order, and uniquely number each student. Use a random number generator on a calculator to select 100 students.

_____

_____

_____

_____

d Choose the first 100 students to arrive in the cafeteria at lunch time.

_____

_____

_____

_____

e Put the names of the Year 11 students in a hat and randomly select 100 of them by pulling names from the hat.

_____

_____

_____

_____

2 Niall is asked to investigate this hypothesis:

'Girls in Year 7 know their times tables better than boys do.'

There are 200 Year 7 students in his school, which is too many for him to survey individually.

Describe how he could select a sample of students from Year 7.

_____

_____

_____

_____

_____

3 Sue is asked to investigate this hypothesis:

'Students who travel to school by bus spend less time, on average, doing homework than other students do.'

There are over 1000 students in the school.

Sue surveys 50 students who travel by bus.

Is this a sensible approach?

Give a reason for your answer.

_____

_____

_____

_____

_____

_____

_____

4 The table shows information about 250 workers in a factory.

	Number of workers
Male	120
Female	130

a Work out the fraction who are male.

_____

_____

b Work out the percentage who are male.

_____

_____

A sample of 75 workers is taken using the same proportions of males and females.

c How many male workers are there in the sample?

_____

_____

_____

_____

_____

_____

Revision papers

Paper 1 ✄

Name _____   **Date** _____

1   Express 360 as the product of its prime factors.

_____

_____

_____

_____

_____

_____

_____

(2 marks)

2   Amir is 18 years older than Joy.

Joy is four times as old as Ben.

The sum of their three ages is 72.

Find the ratio of the ages of Ben to Joy to Amir.

_____

_____

_____

_____

_____

_____

_____

_____

_____

(4 marks)

3 *ABCD* is a parallelogram.

ADE is a straight line.

F is the point on *CD* such that *BFE* is a straight line.

Angle *BFC* is 28°.

Angle *BAD* is 128°.

Show that angle *DEF* is 24°.

Give reasons for each stage of your working.

_____

_____

_____

_____

_____

(3 marks)

4 The tip of the minute hand is 12 cm from the centre of a clock.

The tip of the hour hand is 8 cm from the centre of the clock.

James says that in 1 hour, the distance travelled by the tip of the minute hand is 18 times the distance travelled by the tip of the hour hand.

Is he correct?

You must show all your working.

_____

_____

_____

_____

_____

(4 marks)

5 **a** Rotate the flag *F* 180° about the origin.

   Label the new flag *A*.   (1 mark)

b Reflect flag *A* in the *x*-axis.
   Label the new flag *B*.   (1 mark)

c Describe the single transformation that
   moves Flag *F* to Flag *B*.

_____

_____

_____

(2 marks)

6 The diagram shows an isosceles triangle.

All measurements are in centimetres.

The perimeter of the triangle is 100 cm.

Show that $y = 18$.

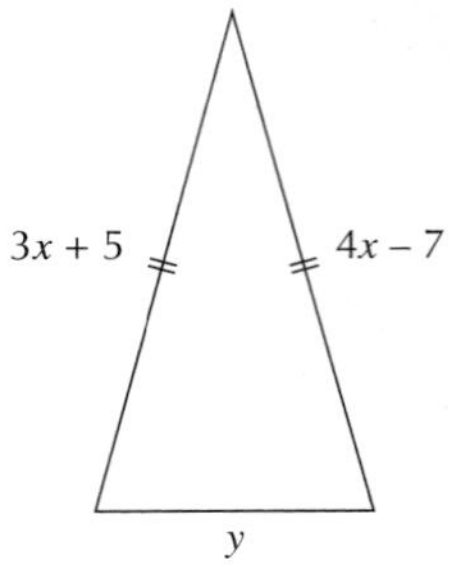

$3x + 5$ $\qquad$ $4x - 7$

y

_____

_____

_____

_____

_____

(4 marks)

7 **a** Show that a line with the equation $y = 4x + 3$ is not parallel to the line with equation $2y = 4x - 6$.

_____

_____

(1 mark)

b Write an equation of a line that is parallel to $y = 4x + 3$.

_____

_____

(1 mark)

8 The mean time it takes for 28 students to walk to school is 10.5 minutes.

The mean time for the 16 boys in the class is 10 minutes.

Show that the mean time for the girls is 11.2 minutes.

_____

_____

_____

_____

_____

(3 marks)

9 The price of a new TV is £540. This price includes VAT at 20%.

What was the price of the TV before VAT was added?

_____

_____

_____

_____

(2 marks)

10 The graph of $y = x^2 + 2x - 1$ is drawn on the grid.

a Use the graph to estimate the solution to $x^2 + 2x - 1 = 0$.

_____

_____

(2 marks)

b By drawing a straight line on the grid, solve the equation $x^2 + 2x - 1 = 2$.

_____

_____

_____

_____

(2 marks)

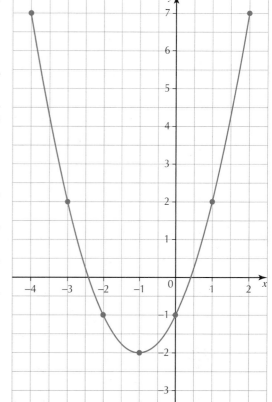

11 Write these numbers in order of size.

Start with the smallest.

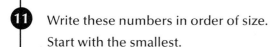

3.15̇3̇   3.153̇   3.1̇53̇   3.153

_____

_____

(2 marks)

12 Two gold-coloured statues look identical.

Only one is made from gold.

Each statue has a volume of approximately $26 \, cm^3$.

The density of gold is $19.6 \, g/cm^3$.

Statue A weighs just under a kilogram.

Statue B weighs approximately half a kilogram.

Which statue is the fake?

You must show your working.

_____

_____

_____

_____

_____

(4 marks)

13 **a** Write the value of $144^{\frac{1}{2}}$.

_____

(1 mark)

b Find the value of $64^{\frac{2}{3}}$.

_____

_____

(2 marks)

c Work out the value of $(3.12 \times 10^6) \div (4 \times 10^{-3})$

Give your answer in standard form.

_____

_____

(2 marks)

14 3 coffees and 4 buns cost £9.50.

4 coffees and 2 buns cost £10.

Work out the cost of 2 coffees and 3 buns.

_____

_____

_____

_____

_____

(4 marks)

15 The table shows information about the times taken by some students to complete a Maths task.

	Time
Least time	1 minute 40 seconds
Median	3 minutes 30 seconds
Lower quartile	3 minutes 10 seconds
Interquartile range	30 seconds
Range	3 minutes 10 seconds

a Draw a box plot for the information above.

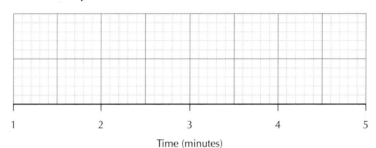

Time (minutes)

(3 marks)

The box plot below shows information about a group of teachers doing the same Maths task.

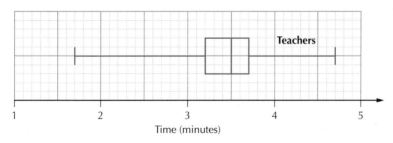

Time (minutes)

b Compare the distributions of times of the students with the distribution of times of the teachers.

_____

_____

_____

_____

(2 marks)

x	1	2	3	4
y	12	3	$1\frac{1}{3}$	$\frac{3}{4}$

y is inversely proportional to x^2.

Find the positive value of x when $y = 48$.

_____

_____

_____

_____

_____

(3 marks)

17 The diagram shows right-angled triangle ABC.

All lengths are in centimetres.

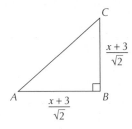

a Write the length of AC in as simple terms as possible.

_____

_____

(2 marks)

b The area of triangle ABC is $9\,cm^2$.

Work out the value of x.

_____

_____

_____

_____

(2 marks)

Paper 2

Name _____ **Date** _____

1 Solve $4x + 5 = 2(x + 5)$

_____

_____

_____

(3 marks)

2 A logo uses a circle of radius 50 cm as shown.

Gold paint and silver paint are used to cover equal sectors.

a Work out the area of one sector.

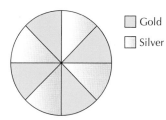

☐ Gold
☐ Silver

_____

_____

_____

_____

_____

(2 marks)

A new logo is designed, as shown.

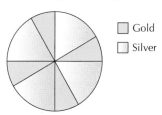

☐ Gold
☐ Silver

b Each silver sector now covers twice as much area as each gold sector.

Work out the arc length of one silver sector.

_____

_____

_____

_____

(4 marks)

3 Lily buys a multipack of crisps for £2.10.

At a charity event. she sells all 12 packs for 30p each.

Lily says she will make more than 70% profit.

Show that Lily is correct.

_____

_____

_____

_____

(3 marks)

4 In a car park, there are only red cars, white cars and black cars.

There are:

- twice as many red cars as white cars
- three times as many black cars as red cars.

Helen said, 'The probability that the next car to leave the car park is white is $\frac{1}{10}$.'

Show that she is incorrect.

_____

_____

_____

_____

(3 marks)

5 **a** $y^2 \times y^x = y^7$

Write the value of x.

_____

(1 mark)

b $(3^3)^y = 3^{12}$

Write the value of y.

_____

(1 mark)

c $10^x \times 1000^y = 10^a$

Show that $a = x + 3y$.

_____

_____

(2 marks)

6 The table shows information about the heights of 20 members of a youth club.

Height, h (cm)	Frequency
$155 < h \leqslant 160$	4
$160 < h \leqslant 165$	9
$165 < h \leqslant 170$	5
$170 < h \leqslant 175$	0
$175 < h \leqslant 180$	2

a Work out an estimate for the mean height of the 20 members of the youth club.

_____

_____

_____

_____

(3 marks)

b Give a reason why the mean might not be the best average to use.

_____

_____

(1 mark)

7 *ABCD* is a trapezium.

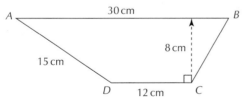

Work out the size of angle *ABC*.

Give your answer to 1 decimal place.

_____

_____

_____

_____

_____

_____

(5 marks)

8 A number x is rounded to 1 decimal place.

The result is 18.7

Using inequalities, write the error interval for x.

_____

_____

(2 marks)

9 Use your calculator to work out:

$$\sqrt{\frac{\tan 15^\circ + \sin 55^\circ}{\cos 55^\circ - \tan 15^\circ}}$$

a Write all the figures on your calculator display.

_____

(2 marks)

b Write your answer to part **a** to 3 significant figures

_____

(1 mark)

10 In this question, assume that each worker works at the same rate.

Last week it took 7 workers $3\frac{1}{2}$ days to construct a wooden building.

This week there are only 5 workers to construct an identical building.

Each worker is paid £110 for each day or part of a day they work.

One of the workers said, 'I will be paid over £500 this week.'

Show that he is correct.

_____

_____

_____

_____

_____

(3 marks)

11 The diagram shows a distance–time graph for a bike ride.

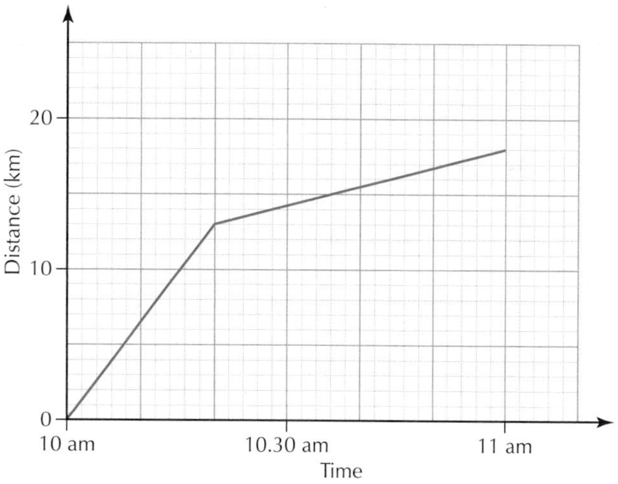

a Between which times does the bike travel at its greatest speed?

_____

_____

(2 marks)

b Work out the greatest speed. Give your answer in km/h.

_____

_____

_____

(2 marks)

12 In the diagram, *AB* and *BC* are two sides of a regular 18-sided polygon.
Work out the size of angle *BCA*.
You must show all your working.

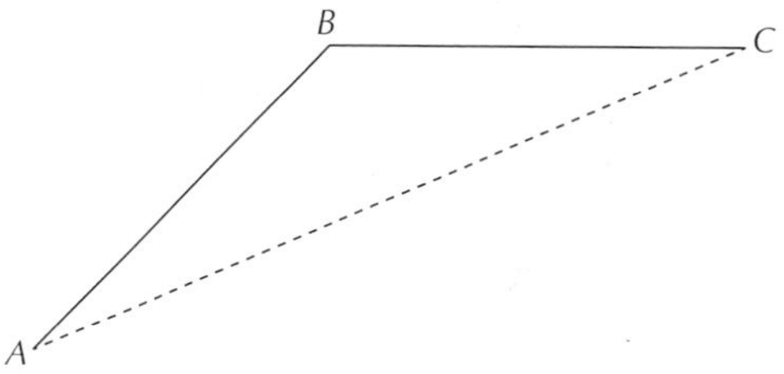

_____

_____

_____

(3 marks)

13 These pie charts show information about the pets owned by the people living in two towns.

Pets owned by people in Chyde

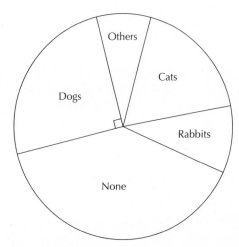

Pets owned by people in Dilby

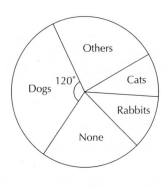

The ratio of the number of people living in Chyde to the number living in Dilby is given by the ratio of the areas of the pie charts.

a Liam said, 'The pie charts show that more people own dogs in Dilby than in Chyde. This is because the sector for dogs has a bigger angle for Dilby.'

Give a reason why his statement might not be true.

_____

_____

_____

(1 mark)

b Estimate the proportion of the total number of people living in the two towns that have dogs.

_____

_____

_____

_____

_____

_____

_____

(3 marks)

14   **a** In February 2010 a man bought a ring for £260.

Each year the value of the ring increased by 3%.

Calculate the value of the ring in February 2018.

_____

_____

_____

_____

(2 marks)

b In February 2015 a woman bought a necklace for £518.

Over 3 years the value of this necklace had increased to £600.

This is equivalent to an increase of approximately x% each year, where x is an integer.

Work out the value of x.

_____

_____

_____

_____

_____

(3 marks)

15   On the grid, show the region that satisfies all these inequalities.

$y \leqslant 5$ $x + y \geqslant 6$ $y \geqslant x - 1$

Label the region R.

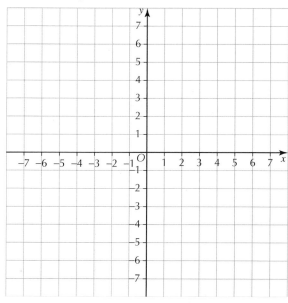

(3 marks)

16 **a** Adam is going to choose a coffee and a cake in a café.

He can choose from 5 different coffees and 10 different cakes.

Eve tells him there are 15 different ways of choosing a coffee and cake.

Is Eve correct?

You must give a reason for your answer.

_____

_____

(2 marks)

b 10 teams enter a competition.

Each team plays every other team twice.

Work out the total number of games played in the competition.

_____

_____

_____

_____

(2 marks)

17 Solve $(x - 3)^2 = 5$.

Give your solution to 3 significant figures.

_____

_____

_____

(2 marks)

Paper 3 ✖

Name _____   **Date** _____

1 Solve the simultaneous equations.

$4x - y = 2$

$x + y = 1$

_____

_____

_____

_____

(3 marks)

2 A supermarket sells beans in tins of three sizes.

Small   250 g for   65p

Medium   275 g for   85p

Large   350 g for   £1.05

Which size is the best buy?

_____

_____

_____

_____

(3 marks)

3 A concrete block has a volume of 1.9 m³.

The mass of the block is 4560 kg.

Work out the density of the concrete in g/cm³.

_____

_____

_____

_____

(3 marks)

4 The table shows the prices of a cup of coffee in different shops.

Price of a cup of coffee (£)	Number of shops
1.80	1
1.85	2
1.90	2
2.30	3

a What is the modal price of a cup of coffee?

_____

(1 mark)

b Find the median price of a cup of coffee.

_____

_____

(1 mark)

c Carl says the mean price of a cup of coffee is £2.05.

Is he correct?

You must show your working.

_____

_____

_____

_____

(2 marks)

5 A tunnel is 500 m long.

A train 130 m long passes completely through the tunnel at 90 km/h.

How long does it take the train to pass completely through the tunnel?

Give your answer in seconds.

_____

_____

_____

_____

(4 marks)

6 A farmer has 840 animals.

He has cows, sheep, pigs and chickens.

Two-fifths of his animals are sheep.

15% of his animals are chickens.

The ratio of the number of cows to the number of pigs is 5:4

Work out the number of cows he has.

_____

_____

_____

_____

_____

_____

_____

(5 marks)

7 Find the reciprocal of $2\frac{2}{3}$.

Give your answer as a decimal.

_____

_____

(1 mark)

8 The side length of a square is 5.8 cm, measured to 1 decimal place.

Amil says that the error interval of the area of the square is $33\,\text{cm}^2 \leqslant \text{area} < 34\,\text{cm}^2$

By working out the correct error interval, show that he is not correct.

_____

_____

_____

(3 marks)

9 The angles of a triangle are $x°$, $2x°$ and $5x°$.

What is the value of x?

_____

_____

(2 marks)

10 A florist has roses and carnations in the ratio 2:1.

The florist has red, pink and yellow roses in the ratio 6:3:1.

The florist has 120 carnations.

How many red roses does the florist have?

_____

_____

_____

(3 marks)

11 **a** A cylindrical can, radius 4 cm, has a volume of 340 cm³.

Work out the area of the curved surface of the can.

_____

_____

_____

_____

_____

(3 marks)

b A rectangle has a perimeter of 52 cm and an area of 144 cm².

Show that the length of the diagonal of the rectangle is approximately 20 cm.

_____

_____

_____

_____

(3 marks)

12 $m = 5 \times 10^{-6}$ and $n = 4.3 \times 10^{8}$

Calculate the values of each of the following.

Give your answers in standard form.

a mn _____

(1 mark)

b m^3 _____

(1 mark)

c $\dfrac{1}{m} + n$ _____

(1 mark)

13 Ben, Mae and Laz play a game in which they roll a small toy animal.

It lands on its feet, its side or its back.

Ben, Mae and Laz roll the animal a number of times.

The table shows the results.

	Ben	Mae	Laz
Feet	26	49	13
Side	9	23	6
Back	4	8	1

a Whose results give the best estimate for the probability that the animal will land on its feet?

Give a reason for your answer.

_____

_____

_____

_____

(1 mark)

b Use **all** the results in the table to work out an estimate for the probability that in two rolls the animal will land on its feet on the first roll and on its side on the second roll.

Give your answer to 3 decimal places.

_____

_____

_____

_____

_____

_____

(2 marks)

14 An investment increases in value by 4% each year.

a Bert says, 'It will take 20 years for the value of the investment to double.'

Is he correct?

Explain your answer.

_____

_____

_____

_____

(2 marks)

b At a restaurant a 20% service charge is automatically added to the bill.

Customers can then add extra to the bill as a tip.

Jim's food bill was £30 before the service charge was added.

Altogether he paid £40.32.

What percentage did he add to the bill as a tip?

_____

_____

_____

_____

(3 marks)

15 At a school fête tickets are chosen at random from a drum.

Tickets with a number ending in a 3 or 7 win a prize.

There is a probability of 0.3 of choosing a winning ticket.

a What is the probability of choosing a ticket that does **not** win a prize?

_____

(1 mark)

b There are **fewer than** 100 winning tickets in the drum.

Work out the greatest possible number of tickets in the drum.

_____

_____

_____

_____

(3 marks)

16 The histogram shows some information about 200 tomatoes.

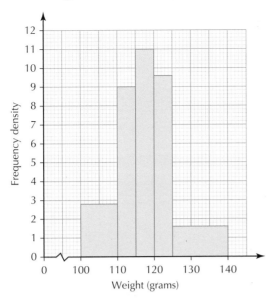

a Show that one half of the tomatoes weigh between 110 g and 120 g.

_____

_____

_____

_____

_____

_____

_____

(3 marks)

b Show that 8% of the tomatoes weigh more than 130 g.

_____

_____

_____

_____

_____

(2 marks)

17 The cumulative frequency graph shows information about the waiting times to see a doctor in a hospital on one day.

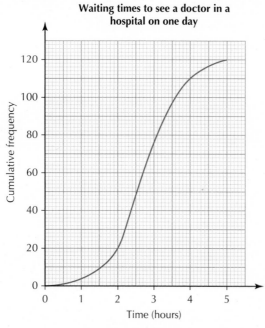

a Use the graph to find an estimate for the median time waiting.

_____

_____

_____

(1 mark)

b Mo says the interquartile range of the waiting time is 96 minutes.

Is she correct? You must give a reason for your answer.

_____

_____

_____

_____

_____

_____

(3 marks)

Formulae you should know

These are the formulae that you need to learn for your GCSE (9–1) Maths exam.

Area and perimeter

Area of rectangle = $l \times w$

Perimeter of rectangle = $2l + 2w$

Area of parallelogram = $b \times h$

Perimeter of parallelogram = $2a + 2b$

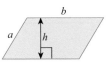

Triangle = $\frac{1}{2} b \times h$

Area of trapezium = $\frac{1}{2}(a \times b)h$

Circles

Circumference =
$\pi \times$ diameter, $C = \pi d$

Circumference =
$2 \times \pi \times$ radius, $C = 2\pi r$

Area of a circle =
$\pi \times$ radius squared, $A = \pi r^2$

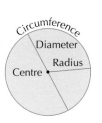

Volumes

Cuboid = $l \times w \times h$

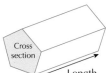

Prism = area of cross section $\times$ length

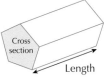

Cylinder = $\pi r^2 h$

Pythagoras' theorem

For a right-angled triangle,
$a^2 + b^2 = c^2$

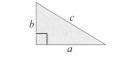

Trigonometric ratios (*new to F*)

$\sin x° = \dfrac{\text{opp}}{\text{hyp}}$, $\cos x° = \dfrac{\text{adj}}{\text{hyp}}$,

$\tan x° = \dfrac{\text{opp}}{\text{adj}}$

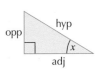

Compound measures

Speed

$\text{speed} = \dfrac{\text{distance}}{\text{time}}$

Density

$\text{density} = \dfrac{\text{mass}}{\text{volume}}$

Compound interest

Where *P* is the principal amount, *r* is the interest rate over a given period and *n* is number of times that the interest is compounded:

$\text{Total accrued} = P\left(1 + \dfrac{r}{100}\right)^n$

Higher tier formulae

pyramid
$= \dfrac{1}{3} \times$ area of base $\times h$

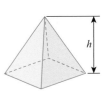

Quadratic equations

The quadratic formula

The solutions of $ax^2 + bx + c = 0$,

where $a \neq 0$, are given by $x = \dfrac{-b \pm \sqrt{(b^2 - 4ac)}}{2a}$

Trigonometric formulae

Area of triangle $= \frac{1}{2} ab \sin C$

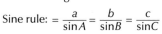

In **any** triangle where ABC where a, b and c are lengths of the sides:

Sine rule: $= \dfrac{a}{\sin A} = \dfrac{b}{\sin B} = \dfrac{c}{\sin C}$

Cosine rule:

$a^2 = b^2 + c^2 - 2bc \cos A$

Probability

Where $P(A)$ is the probability of outcome A and $P(B)$ is the probability of outcome B:

$P(A$ or $B) = P(A) + P(B) - P(A$ and $B)$

$P(A$ and $B) = P(A$ given B$)$ $P(B)$

Notes

Notes

Answers

1.1 Rounding and limits of accuracy

1 a 150   **b** 52.5

2 a 8.4999.....   **b** 64.999...

3 5004.99....... grams

4 a i 74   **ii** 40

   b i 75.9999 (upper bound = 76)

     ii 41.9999 (upper bound = 42)

5 a 3.645   **b** 3.65499.... (upper bound 3.655)

6 a 0.3077   **b** 0.3175

7 a $4.195 \leqslant x + y < 4.305$

   b $3.095 \leqslant x - y < 3.205$

   c $1.98925 \leqslant xy < 2.08125$

8 a $15.75 \, \text{cm}^2$ **b** $24.75 \, \text{cm}^2$

9 A, as the error interval is 4.995 metres $\leqslant$ height of lorry $<$ 5.005 metres

1.2 Prime factors, LCM and HCF

1 $2 \times 2 \times 5 \times 5$ or $2^2 \times 5^2$

2 $2^3 \times 3^2 \times 7$

3 84

4 12

5 a $3^2 \times 5^4 \times 7^2$ or 275625   **b** $3 \times 5^3 \times 7$ or 2625

6 4 packs of burgers and three packs of bread buns

7 5 days

8 1350

1.3 Indices, roots and surds

1 a 1   **b** 8   **c** 343

   d 0.2   **e** 0.0625   **f** 0.001

2 a 7^5 **b** 7^4 **c** 7^3

   d 7^2 **e** 7^{-2} **f** 7^{-7}

3 6 and 7

4 a $\sqrt{10}$ **b** $5\sqrt{2}$ **c** $4\sqrt{3}$

   d $\sqrt{2}$ **e** $\dfrac{\sqrt{6}}{\sqrt{3}}$ or $\dfrac{\sqrt{2}}{\sqrt{3}}$

5 a 6   **b** 3   **c** 0.77 or $\dfrac{1}{13}$

6 25

7 a 6^6 **b** 6^{12} **c** 6^3

8 a $2\sqrt{6}$ **b** $3\sqrt{2}$ **c** $6\sqrt{5}$

9 $\dfrac{7}{20}$ or 0.35

10 6

1.4 Fractions and mixed numbers

1 a $4\dfrac{31}{40}$ **b** $\dfrac{13}{20}$ **c** $10\dfrac{5}{7}$

2 $\dfrac{7}{24}$

3 £30

4 40

5 94

1.5 Standard form

1 0.00653

2 a 7.5×10^5 **b** 7.97×10^7

   c 1.5×10^{11} **d** 3×10^4

3 7.36×10^{-21} grams

4 4×10^5

5 a Mercury   **b** 2.78×10^4 miles

   c No, not correct. Although generally true, it does not work for Venus and Mars. Mars is further away from the Sun than Venus, but Venus has a larger diameter than Mars.

6 a 1.445×10^8 **b** 111 or 112

1.6 Recurring decimals to fractions

1

0.101	→	0.101010
0.10$\dot{1}$		0.101111
0.1$\dot{0}$$\dot{1}$		0.101101
0.$\dot{1}$0$\dot{1}$		0.101000

2 $0.735, 0.7\dot{3}\dot{5}, 0.73\dot{5}, 0.\dot{7}3\dot{5}$

3 a $0.\dot{3}$ **b** $0.1\dot{6}$ **c** $0.8\dot{3}$

4 $0.8, 0.88, 0.888, 0.\dot{8}$

5 a Dividing 1 by 3 gives $\dfrac{1}{3} = 0.\dot{3}$. One-third is a recurring decimal so it cannot be written as a terminating decimal.

6 a $\dfrac{2}{9}$ **b** $\dfrac{6}{11}$

7 Show or state that $0.\dot{6}$ is $\dfrac{2}{3}$ then show $\dfrac{2}{3} \times 6 = 4$.

ANSWERS TO CHAPTER 2: ALGEBRA

2.1 Factorisation

1 a $(t-1)(t+1)$ **b** $(w-8)(w+8)$ **c** $(x-6)(x+6)$

2 a $(x+3)(x+4)$ **b** $(x+6)(x+2)$ **c** $(y-4)(y+6)$

3 a $(2x-3)(2x+3)$ **b** $(4-x)(4+x)$ **c** $(5x-2)(5x+2)$

4 a $\left(x+\dfrac{1}{2}\right)\left(x-\dfrac{1}{2}\right)$ **b** $\left(y-\dfrac{1}{4}\right)\left(y+\dfrac{1}{4}\right)$ **c** $\left(2t-\dfrac{1}{3}\right)\left(2t+\dfrac{1}{3}\right)$

5 a $(x-2)(x-16)$ **b** $(x-9)(x+8)$ **c** $(x-4)^2$

6 The answer should be $(5x+1)(3x-1)$.

7 $n^2+3n+2 = (n+1)(n+2)$

If n is odd, $(n+1)$ is even, $(n+2)$ is odd, and even $\times$ odd = even.

If n is even $(n+1)$ is odd, $(n+2)$ is even and odd $\times$ even = even.

So $(n+1)(n+2)$ will always be the product of an odd number and an even number, so is always even.

2.2 Setting up and solving linear equations

1 a $2x+8 = 32$ or $4x+16 = 64$ **b** 12

2 4

3 12

4 36

5 60 km/h

6 $6x-1 = 2x+3 \Rightarrow 4x = 4 \Rightarrow x = 1$; length of sloping side = 5 cm, base = 6 cm. Using Pythagoras' theorem, $5^2 = h^2 + 3^2$ so $h^2 = 16$ and $h = 4$.

The area is $\dfrac{1}{2} \times 6 \times 4 = 12\,\text{cm}^2$

7 7.9 km (1 d.p.)

2.3 Solving quadratic equations by factorising

1 a $-4, -6$ **b** $-5, -4$

c $2, -3$ **d** $1, 5$

2 a $(x+5)(x-5) = 0$

$\qquad x = 5$ or $x = -5$

$\qquad x^2 = 25$

$\qquad x = \pm 5$

b $\qquad x^2 = 25$

$\qquad \sqrt{x^2} = \pm\sqrt{25}$

$\qquad x = 5$

3 a $-\dfrac{1}{2}, 3$ **b** $-\dfrac{1}{3}, -1$

c $-\dfrac{3}{4}, \dfrac{1}{5}$ **d** $-\dfrac{1}{3}, \dfrac{1}{2}$

4 a $-\dfrac{5}{2}, \dfrac{5}{2}$ **b** $-\dfrac{3}{5}, \dfrac{3}{5}$

c $-\dfrac{5}{4}, \dfrac{5}{4}$ **d** $-\dfrac{1}{30}, \dfrac{1}{30}$

5 $x = -2$ or $x = -1$

6 a $-\dfrac{2}{3}, \dfrac{1}{2}$ **b** $\dfrac{3}{2}, \dfrac{5}{4}$

7 13 m by 17 m

2.4 Solving quadratic equations by completing the square

1 $(x+4)^2 - 19 = x^2 + 8x + 16 - 19$

$\qquad\qquad\qquad\quad = x^2 + 8x - 3$

2 a $(x-3)^2 - 9 = -5$

$\qquad (x-3)^2 = 4$

$\qquad x-3 = 2$ or $x-3 = -2$

$\qquad x = 5$ or $x = 1$

b Factorising $x^2 - 6x + 5 = 0$, gives $(x-5)(x+1) = 0$, so $x-5 = 0$ or $x+1 = 0$, leading to $x = 5$ and $x = -1$.

3 a $(x+3)^2 - 5$ **b** $(x-9)^2 - 83$ **c** $(x-2)^2 - 3$

2.5 Changing the subject of a formula

1 a $t = \dfrac{A-5}{m}$ **b** $t = \sqrt{\dfrac{k}{w}}$ **c** $t = \dfrac{4H+3}{5}$

d $t = \dfrac{8+p}{p}$ **e** $t = \dfrac{1}{m-1}$ **f** $t = \sqrt[3]{\dfrac{k}{4}}$

2 a $r = \sqrt{\dfrac{A}{4\pi}}$ **b** $r = \sqrt[3]{\dfrac{3V}{4\pi}}$ **c** $r = \dfrac{wk^2}{4\pi^2}$

3 a $v = \sqrt{\dfrac{2E}{m}}$ **b** $v = \dfrac{3d}{mk}$ **c** $v = d(t-a) + 1$

4 a Line 2 should be $yx = 18w - 18x$, then line 3 should be $yx + 18x = 18w$.

b $x = \dfrac{18w}{y+18}$

5 a $x = \dfrac{8-y}{8}$ **b** $x = \dfrac{6y+3}{2}$ **c** $x = \dfrac{qt+mp}{q-m}$

2.6 Using the nth term to generate sequences

1 a $\dfrac{n+(n-1)}{n+(n+1)} = \dfrac{2n-1}{2n+1}$ **b** $\dfrac{3n+2}{4n+4}$

c $-\dfrac{5n-1}{105-5n}$ **d** $-\dfrac{2(n+(n-1))}{5n+2(n-1)} = \dfrac{2-4n}{7n-2}$

2 a

b $4n+1$

c Pattern 29 (assuming that you did not use them to make the earlier patterns in the sequence)

3 2, 7, 12, 17, 22: Nav started at the 0th term.

4 7, 4, 1, –2, –5

5 a $109 - 9n$ **b** $1 - 0.1n$

6 Show that nth term is $\dfrac{\sqrt{n}}{n + 10}$, so when $n = 100$,

this is $\dfrac{\sqrt{100}}{110} = \dfrac{10}{110} = \dfrac{1}{11}$.

7 $3n - 8$

8 Show that nth term is $\dfrac{n + 3}{4n - 3}$, then the product of

17th and 18th terms is:

$\dfrac{17 + 3}{(4 \times 17) - 3} \times \dfrac{18 + 3}{(4 \times 18) - 3} = \dfrac{20}{65} \times \dfrac{21}{69} = \dfrac{4}{13} \times \dfrac{7}{23} = \dfrac{28}{299}$

2.7 Linear inequalities

1 $0 \leqslant x \leqslant 5$

2 a 12   **b** 0

3 13, 17, 19, 23, 29, 31, 37, 41, 43, 47

4

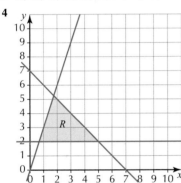

5 a $x > -1$ **b** $t \leqslant \dfrac{1}{2}$ **c** $x \geqslant 4$

2.8 Finding the equation of a straight line

1 a 4   **b** $y = 4x + 1$

2 $y = 2x + 3$

3 a $y = 3x - 7$ **b** $y = 2x - 1$

4 $y = 3x - 5$

5 a –2   **b** $y = 8 - 2x$

6 For example, shows that the gradient of AB and BC are both $\dfrac{1}{3}$ and, as they pass through the same point B, they must be on the same line.

7 No he is not correct. The equation of the line is $y = 11 - 2x$.

2.9 Drawing quadratic graphs and using them to solve equations

1 a

x	–2	–1	0	1	2
y	4	–3	–4	1	12

b

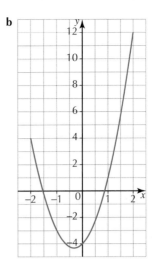

c Solution is where the graph intercepts the x-axis

d –1.5

2 a By drawing the straight line $y = 6$ and finding the x-coordinates of the intersection with the graph given

b $x = -1$ or $x = 4$

3 a i $x = -1.4$ or $x = 3.5$ **ii** $x = -2$ or $x = 4$

  b i $y = 2$ **ii** $x = -1.8$ or $x = 3.8$

2.10 Recognising the shapes of graphs

1 $y = x^3$ is graph D.

2 $y = \dfrac{1}{x}$ is graph G.

3 $y = x^2 - 4$ is graph C.

4 $y = 3x - x^2$ is graph I.

5 $x + y = 7$ is graph A.

6 $y = x^3 + 4$ is graph E.

7 $y = \sin x$ is graph B.

8 $y = 2^x$ is graph F.

9 $y = \cos x$ is graph H.

2.11 Trigonometric graphs

1 a 0   **b** 1
  c –1   **d** 1
  e 0   **f** –1

2 Draw the line $y = 0.5$ on the graph: there are two intersections between the curve and the line, meaning there are two solutions.

3 On one graph, draw the line $x = 45$ and see where it intersects the graph, then draw a horizontal line from this to the other graph; this will also intersect at $x = 45$ on that graph. Hence $\sin 45° = \cos 45°$.

On each graph, draw the line $x = 45$ and show that they intersect the graph at the same y-value, which could be implied by a statement about symmetry of the graphs.

4 a 53° and 127°   **b** 204° and 335°
  c 57° and 303°   **d** 95° and 265°

2.12 Simultaneous equations

1 a $x = 2, y = -3$ **b** $x = 1, y = -5$ **c** $x = -2, y = 11$

2 Tea costs £1.65, coffee costs £2.40.

3 He did not multiply the bracket out correctly, so line 4 of the solution should have been $6x - 14 + 16x = 41$.

He also added 7 to 41 to give 49 instead of 48.

(So, $x = \dfrac{5}{2}$; $y = -13$)

4 David is 40, his daughter is 15. $x + 10 = 2y + 20$ and $x - 10 = 6y - 60$

5

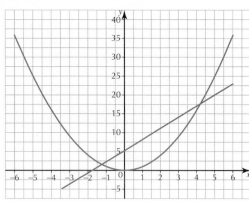

$x = -1.2$ and $x = 4.2$

2.13 Equations of circles and their graphs

1 a

x	-2	-1.5	-1	-0.5	0	0.5	1	1.5	2
y	0	±1.3	±1.7	±1.9	±2	±1.9	±1.7	±1.3	0

b When $y^2 = 0$ then $y = 0$, giving one value.

When $y^2 \neq 0$ then there are two values, from the positive and negative square roots.

c i

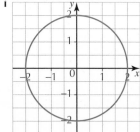

ii The radius is 2.

2 a

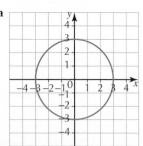

b The radius is 3.

3 The equation of a circle radius r, is given by $x^2 + y^2 = r^2$, so $r^2 = 16$, giving radius 4.

2.14 Working with algebraic fractions

1 a $x = 8$ **b** $x = 12$ **c** $x = 7$

2 The mistake is in the first line of her solution. It should be:

$\dfrac{x}{7} = 1 + 3$

$x = 28$

3 a $x = 7$ **b** $x = 3$ **c** $x = 1.5$

4 a $x = 3$ **b** $x = 2$ **c** $x = -5$

5 The second line should be $6x + 3 = 5x - 5$, giving $x = -8$.

6 a $x + 1$ **b** $\dfrac{1}{x - 2}$

7 a $\dfrac{1}{x^2 - 1}$ or $\dfrac{1}{(x - 1)(x + 1)}$ **b** 2 metres

c $\dfrac{4x}{x^2 - 1}$ or $\dfrac{4x}{(x - 1)(x + 1)}$ $= \dfrac{4 \times 2}{2^2 - 1} = \dfrac{8}{3}$

2.15 Plotting and interpreting $y = k^x$

1 a

x	0	1	2	3
$y = 2^x$	1	2	4	8

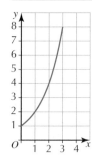

b $x = 2.6$

2 a Each day she puts double the amount of the previous day. On 3 December she put £4 into the bag, so on 4 December, she will put £4 × 2 = £8.

b Each day the amount doubles from the previous day, so on 11 December there would be £1 × 2 × 2 × 2 × 2 × 2 × 2... up to 2^{10} (or £1024) on the 11th day.

c £8 388 608

2.16 Functions

1 a 9 **b** 21 **c** 7.5

2 a 19 **b** -125 **c** 13.4

3 a $-\dfrac{1}{4}$ **b** 32 **c** $x = \dfrac{1}{2}$

4 a 10 **b** -1.5 **c** 2 **d** 4

ANSWERS TO CHAPTER 3: RATIO, PROPORTION AND RATES OF CHANGE

3.1 Simplifying ratios, and ratios as fractions

1 a 3:8 **b** 9:2 **c** 7:18

d 18:35:6 **e** 4:7:11 **f** 13:91:41

2 a 1:7 **b** 20:7 **c** 1:5

d 1:10 **e** 2:7 **f** 15:7

3 a i $\frac{8}{15}$ girls; $\frac{7}{15}$ boys   **ii** 15

b i $\frac{6}{11}$ girls; $\frac{5}{11}$ boys   **ii** 11

c i $\frac{7}{8}$ girls; $\frac{1}{8}$ boys   **ii** 8

d i $\frac{3}{7}$ girls; $\frac{4}{7}$ boys   **ii** 7

e i $\frac{7}{10}$ girls; $\frac{3}{10}$ boys   **ii** 10

f i $\frac{9}{13}$ girls; $\frac{4}{13}$ boys   **ii** 13

4 24:26:25

5 a 4:3

b Yes. It is a multiple of 7, the ratio total.

6 3 years, 24 years and 44 years or 6 years, 48 years and 88 years.

7 a 50 g, 100 g, 250 g

b Yes. The total mass is: 50 g + 100 g + 250 g = 400 g.

c 2:4:9

3.2 Dividing a quantity in a given ratio

1 a 150 g and 850 g

b 0.54 m and 0.06 m or 54 cm and 6 cm

c £3.80 and £1.20

d 7 cm, 28 cm and 14 cm

e 120 ml, 180 ml and 700 ml

f 150 g, 75 g and 25 g

2 a F: 93p and £6.82 **b** T

c F: 176 yards and 1584 yards **d** F: 960 g and 1040 g

e T **f** F: £250, £425 and £575

3 a 91 **b** 234

4 a £50, £65 and £85 **b** £17.50

5 240 girls

6 a 210 g flour and 300 g sugar **b** 750 g

c 525 g flour, 600 g butter and 750 g sugar

d 1875 g

7 a No, needs 225 ml of thinner, 1350 ml of red paint and 675 ml of yellow paint. She does not have enough thinner or red paint.

b 2083 ml of orange paint (1250 ml red paint, 625 ml yellow paint and 208 ml thinner)

8 a 8 years old, 11 years old and 16 years old

b £64, £88 and £128

3.3 Using ratio

1 a 1:4 **b** 1:2 **c** 1:$\frac{5}{2}$ **d** 1:$\frac{100}{63}$

e 1:$\frac{9}{40}$ **f** 1:$\frac{130}{77}$

2 a $\frac{19}{11}$ **b** 16 **c** 32 **d** $\frac{5}{17}$ **e** $\frac{27}{2}$ **f** $\frac{25}{2}$

3 He is not correct. Jayden divides 250 m by 100 but he should have divided by 1000 (there are 1000 m in 1 km).

1 cm : 25 000 cm

1 cm : 250 m

1 cm : 0.25 km

4 cm : 1 km

4 a 120 g **b** 320 g

5 a 0.125:1 **b** 7 **c** 5

6 a 2 cm to 1 km and 4 cm to 1 km

b 2.5 km and 1.25 km

7 a 5:6:3:6 **b** 520:295:354:177:354

c 11:12:6:11

3.4 Best-buy problems

1 a 32p and 37.5p, so apples at £1.60 for 5 are the better value

b Approximately 12p and 17p, so dishwasher tablets at £7 for 58 are the better value

2 a Approximately 45p, 37p and 41p, so toilet rolls at £3.35 for 9 are the best value

b Approximately 1.2p/ml, 1.33p/ml and 1.11p/ml, so shampoo at £5 for 450 ml is the best value

3 a £1.14/kg and £1.00/kg

b 875 g or 0.875 kg and 1000 g or 1 kg

c Potatoes at 70p for 700 g are the better value. Part **a** shows the lower cost/kg and part **b** shows the higher mass/£.

4 Tres Emily 0.31p/ml

Pigeon Daily Care 0.50p/ml

Bossie 1.11p/ml

Tres Emily, not Bossie, is the best deal.

5 $\frac{35}{48}$ = 72.9%, $\frac{59}{80}$ = 73.8%, $\frac{43}{60}$ = 71.7%

His performance across the three tests was similar but not exactly the same.

6 Rover: $8 \times 150\,g = 1200\,g$

$2 \times 1200\,g = 2400\,g$

$\dfrac{2400}{8}\,g = 300\,g$

The shopkeeper is not correct. Woof is the better value. The mistake is in the last line of the calculation for Rover, $\dfrac{2400}{8}\,g = 300\,g$, not $600\,g$.

7 a $524:125$

b In the marathon she ran at $13.9\,km/h$ in the 10K race she ran at $15.8\,km/h$. Her average speed was higher in the 10K race than in the marathon.

3.5 Compound measures

1 a $29\,mph$ **b** 75 miles   **c** $91\,s$

2 a £64.75   **b** £714   **c** £19.80

   d £10.40   **e** 24 hours   **f** 42 hours

3 $2.4\,g/cm^3$

4 a $0.42\ldots\,kg/mm^2$ **b** 96% **c** iii

5 $12:35$

6 a £248.98   **b** £66.24

7 a $0.127\,m^3$ **b** $2173.913\,cm^3$ **c** $7.971\,g/cm^3$

3.6 Compound interest and repeated percentage change

1 a compound   **b** simple   **c** compound

   d simple   **e** simple   **f** compound

2 a £9720.00   **b** £4352.00   **c** £21 703.14

   d £4628.81   **e** £4616.18   **f** £421.88

3 £123.24

4 7 years

5 Northern Bank £3191.96, Southern Bank £3180.00, Western Bank £3271.85.

Mel should bank with Western Bank.

6 4 years

7 $£1000 \times 1.0065^8 = £1053.20$, so interest $=$ £1053.20 − £1000 = £53.20

8 a 0.353% **b** $1\,423\,046$ people

3.7 Reverse percentages

1 a F: 100% is 800   **b** F: 100% is 125   **c** T

   d T   **e** F: 100% is £980   **f** F: 100% is £30

2 150 students

3 $120\% = £63.60$, 20% is $120\% \div 6 = £63.60 \div 6 = £10.60$

4 500

5 a Incorrect. Uses 1.03 twice instead of 1.04 and 1.03.

   b Incorrect. Cannot combine 3% and 4%.

   c Correct.

   d Incorrect. Need to divide by 1.04 and 1.03 and not multiply. Sense check that the old salary should be less than the new salary.

6 $£159 \div 1.06 = £150$, which is a £9 increase in price. The customer is incorrect.

7 £6000

8 $1.1 \times 1.3 = 1.43$

3.8 Direct and inverse proportion

1 a D   **b** N   **c** D

   d I   **e** I   **f** D

2 a £4.35   **b** £6.50   **c** £2.97

   d £14.40

3 a 15.75 litres   **b** 360 miles

   c The car uses petrol at a constant rate.

4 a $1.8\,kg$ of butter   **b** 6

   c 2 fewer as Al would need 6 cakes instead of 8.

5 a $S \propto T$

   $S = kT$

   $30 = 6k$

   $k = 5$

   $S = 5T$

   b $S = 15$ **c** $T = 20$

6 $15 = 75k$ should be $75 = 15k$, leading to $k = 5$ and $P = 5Q$

7 $L \propto \dfrac{1}{M}$

$L = \dfrac{k}{m}$

$7 = \dfrac{k}{4}$

$k = 28$

$L = \dfrac{28}{M}$

When $L = 35$,

$35 = \dfrac{28}{M}$

$M = \dfrac{28}{35}$

$M = 0.8$, so it is true.

8 a €1.25   **b** £380   **c** £0.80

ANSWERS TO CHAPTER 4: GEOMETRY AND MEASURES

4.1 3D shapes and surface area

1 $132\,cm^2$

2 $20\,100\,mm^2$

3 $3.64\,m^2$

4 Surface area is $(2 \times \pi \times 3 \times 1.5 + \pi \times 3 \times 5)\,m^2 = 24\pi\,m^2$.

$24\pi \div 14 = 5.38\ldots$, so at least 6 tins of paint are required.

5 $216\,cm^2$

6 a $235.93\,m$ **b** $109\,000\,m^2$

4.2 3D shapes – volume

1 **a** $17.64\,\text{cm}^3$ **b** $7238.23\,\text{cm}^3$

2 $199.92\,\text{cm}^3$

3 **a** $33.5\,\text{ml}$ **b** $419\,\text{ml}$

4 10^3, 10^2 and 0.25 should be circled.

5 Volume of cylinder is $\pi \times 10^2 \times 10\,\text{cm}^3 = 1000\pi\,\text{cm}^3$

  Volume of cone is $\frac{1}{3} \times \pi \times 10^2 \times 30\,\text{cm}^3 = 1000\pi\,\text{cm}^3$

6 **a** $13\,500\,\text{cm}^3$ **b** $13\,200\,\text{cm}^3$

4.3 Similarity

1 $x = 25°$, $y = 65°$, $z = 90°$

2 $7.5\,\text{cm}$

3 The fraction used should be $\frac{4}{6}$ not $\frac{6}{4}$ so the calculation should be $\frac{4}{6} \times 10.5 = 7$

4 **a** $15 \div 5 = 3$, $3 \times 1.5 = 4.5\,\text{cm}$ **b** $123.75\,\text{cm}^2$

5 **a** $16\,\text{cm}$ **b** $2778.75\,\text{cm}^3$

6 No, the area of each face of cube A is $25\,\text{cm}^2$ and each face of cube B is $4\,\text{cm}^2$. The correct ratio is $25 : 4$.

7 **a** T

  b F: if the area of B is $15\,\text{cm}^2$, then the area of A is $9\,\text{cm}^2$.

  c T

  d F: the area of B is $\frac{5}{3}$ of the area of A.

8 $5\,\text{m}$

4.4 Trigonometry

1 $4.1\,\text{cm}$

2 $8.8\,\text{cm}$

3 $7.7 \times \tan 35° = 5.39\ldots$

4 $\dfrac{2}{\sin 68°} = 2.15\ldots = 2.2$

5 **a** $6.93\,\text{m}$ **b** $8.26\,\text{m}$

6 $4.2\,\text{km}$

7 One possible answer is $64 \times \cos 30° + 32 \times \tan 70° = 143.34\ldots = 143\,\text{mm}$

4.5 Arcs and sectors

1 **a** $3.1\,\text{cm}$ **b** $11.1\,\text{cm}$

2 $13.1\,\text{cm}^2$

3 **a** $69.7\,\text{m}^2$ **b** 41.9%

4 He has used $30\,\text{cm}$ instead of $10\,\text{cm}$ for sides HF and GJ.

  He has used area formula instead of arc length formula.

  It should be $20 + 10 + 10 + \dfrac{60}{360} \times 2 \times \pi \times 30$

5 Radius $= 7\,\text{cm}$

  Perimeter of sector is $\left(7 + 7 + \dfrac{1}{10} \times 2 \times \pi \times 7\right)\text{cm} = (14 + 1.4\pi)\,\text{cm}$

  $= (14 + 4.398\ldots)\,\text{cm} = 18.398\,\text{cm} = 18.4\,\text{cm}$

6 $\left(\dfrac{120}{360} \times 400 \times \pi - \dfrac{120}{360} \times 100 \times \pi\right)\text{cm} = 100\pi\,\text{cm}^2$

4.6 Pythagoras' theorem

1 $15.6\,\text{cm}$

2 No, because EG is not the hypotenuse. The formula needs to be written as $13^2 = 12^2 + EG^2$. The correct calculation should be:

$$13^2 = 12^2 + EG^2$$
$$13^2 - 12^2 = EG^2$$
$$EG^2 = 25$$
$$EG = \sqrt{25}$$
$$EG = 5\,\text{cm}$$

3 **a**
$$A^2 = 2^2 + 1.5^2$$
$$A^2 = 6.25$$
$$A = \sqrt{6.25}$$
$$A = 2.5\,\text{m}$$
$$2 \times 2 + 2 \times 1.5 + 2.5 = 9.5\,\text{m}$$

  b 26.3%

4 **a** $6.32\,\text{cm}$ **b** $75.9\,\text{cm}^2$

5 **a** $3.4\,\text{cm}$ **b** $43.6\,\text{cm}$

6 $0.5 \times 2x^2 = 121$
$$x^2 = 121$$
$$x = \sqrt{121}$$
$$x = 11$$
$$A^2 = 11^2 + 22^2$$
$$A^2 = 605$$
$$A = \sqrt{605}$$

7 $1510\,\text{cm}^2$

4.7 Congruent triangles

1 SAS, $AC = FG$, $BC = EF$, angle $ACB =$ angle EFG

2 Not ASA or AAS, angle $GHJ =$ angle KLM, angle $GJH =$ angle KML, but $HJ \neq LM$

3 Yes, for example: SSS, $EF = GH$, $EH = FG$, EG is common to both triangles.

4 Similar triangles, angle $EJH =$ angle FJG, angle $GFJ =$ angle EHJ, angle $FGJ =$ angle JEH, but no corresponding sides are shown as being equal.

5 **a** SAS, $AB = CD$, $BC = DE$, angle $ABC =$ angle CDE

  b 6 triangles, so 15 pairs

6 $8 \times 0.5 \times 6^2 \times \sin 45° = 101.82 \ldots = 102\,\text{cm}^2$ (to 3 s.f.)

4.8 Regular polygons

1 $72°$

2 **a** $135°$ **b** $1080°$

3 **a** $24°$ **b** $156°$

4 **a** Number of sides $= 360° \div$ exterior angle

    Exterior angle $= 180° - 150°$
$$= 30°$$
    Number of sides $= 360° \div 30°$
$$= 12$$

  b $1800°$

5 $17x + x = 180°$ (angles on a straight line add up to 180°)

$\quad\quad 18x = 180°$

$\quad\quad\quad x = 10°$

Number of sides is: $360° \div x = 360° \div 10° = 36$

6 a 9 $\quad\quad\quad\quad$ **b** 140°

4.9 Circle theorems

1 90°, angle in a semicircle

2 15°, angle in a semicircle

3 $s = 90°$, radii meet the tangents at 90°

4 115°, sum of opposite angles of a cyclic quadrilateral is 180°

5 110°, angle at the centre is twice the angle at the circumference, when subtended by the same arc

6 5°, obtuse angle at centre $O = 175°$, radii meet tangents at 90°, angle sum of quadrilateral is 360°

4.10 Translations and vectors

1 a $\begin{pmatrix} 6 \\ -2 \end{pmatrix}$ **b** $\begin{pmatrix} -2 \\ 4 \end{pmatrix}$

2 a

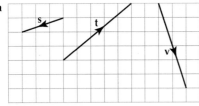

b $s - 2v = \begin{pmatrix} -3 \\ 1 \end{pmatrix} - 2\begin{pmatrix} 2 \\ -6 \end{pmatrix} = \begin{pmatrix} -3 \\ -1 \end{pmatrix} - \begin{pmatrix} 4 \\ -12 \end{pmatrix}$

$\quad\quad\quad = \begin{pmatrix} -7 \\ 11 \end{pmatrix}$

3 a $\overrightarrow{AC} = \mathbf{p} - \mathbf{q}$ $\quad$ **b** $\overrightarrow{OB} = \mathbf{p} + \mathbf{q}$

4 a $\overrightarrow{OT} = \mathbf{a} + 2\mathbf{b}$ $\quad$ **b** $\overrightarrow{VT} = \mathbf{a} + \mathbf{b}$

5 a $\overrightarrow{AB} = \mathbf{b} - \mathbf{a}$ $\quad$ **b** $\overrightarrow{AM} = \frac{1}{2}(\mathbf{b} - \mathbf{a})$

$\quad$ **c** $\overrightarrow{OM} = \frac{1}{2}(\mathbf{a} + \mathbf{b})$

6 a $\begin{pmatrix} 2b \\ a \end{pmatrix} - \begin{pmatrix} a \\ b \end{pmatrix} = \begin{pmatrix} 3 \\ 1 \end{pmatrix}$ Check: $a = 5, b = 4$, gives

$\quad$ $2b - a = 3$ and $a - b = 1$, so correct.

$\quad$ **b** $\mathbf{p} = \begin{pmatrix} 5 \\ 4 \end{pmatrix}, \mathbf{q} = \begin{pmatrix} 8 \\ 5 \end{pmatrix}$

4.11 Rotations

1 a

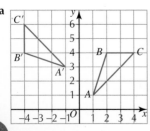

b

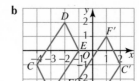

2 a Rotation, 90° anticlockwise, centre of rotation $(-1, 0)$

$\quad$ **b** Rotation, 90° anticlockwise, centre of rotation $(1, 2)$

3 $(0, -2), (-2, -2), (-1, 1)$

4 a

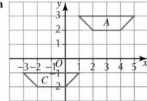

$\quad$ **b** Translation vector $\begin{pmatrix} -4 \\ -4 \end{pmatrix}$

5 a $(0, -3), (-1, -1), (0, 0), (1, -1)$

$\quad$ **b** No:

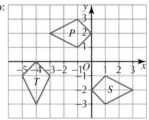

6 $(-x, -y)$

4.12 Reflections

1 a

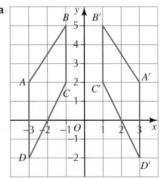

b

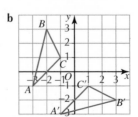

2 a Reflection, line $x = 1$

$\quad$ **b** Reflection, line $y = x$ should be reflection, line $y = -x$

3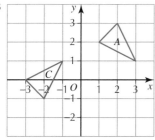

4 $x = -1$, $y = -0.5$

5 Yes: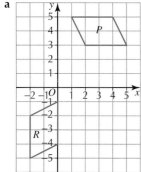

6 a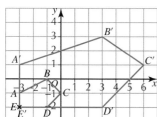

b Rotation, 90° clockwise, centre (−2.5, 2.5)

4.13 Enlargements

1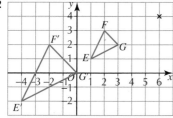

2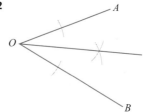

3 The transformation is not correct enlargement. Only two sides of the image correspond to sides of the object.

4 Enlargement, scale factor 3, centre (−3, 2)

5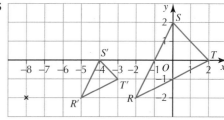

6 a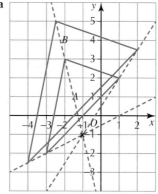

b Scale factor = $\frac{3}{2}$ **c** Scale factor = $\frac{2}{3}$

7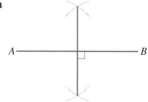

4.14 Constructions

1 a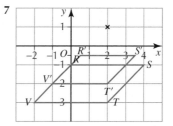

b

2

3 a

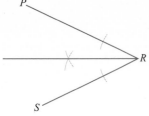

b

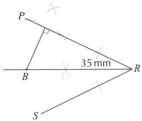

4 a

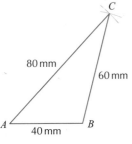

Shown half of
actual size

b

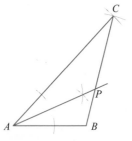

Shown half of
actual size

c 1:2

5 a

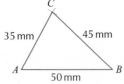

Shown half of
actual size

b

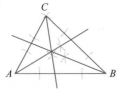

Shown half of
actual size

6

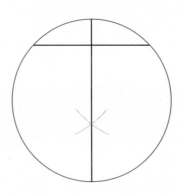

4.15 Loci

1

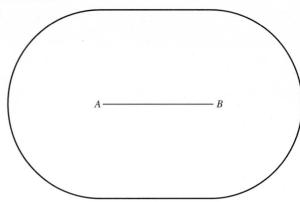

2 a

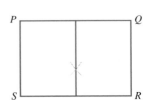

b

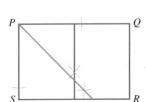

c

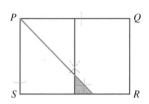

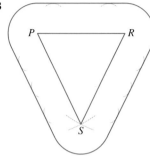

3

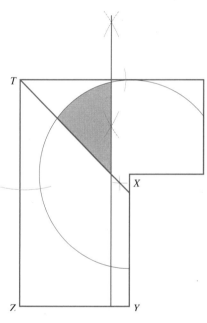

4

5 a

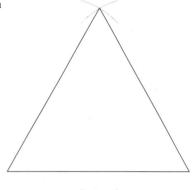

b

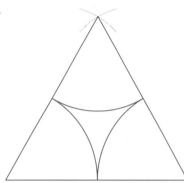

c $\dfrac{1}{2} \times 50^2 \times \sin 60° - 3 \times \dfrac{60}{360} \times \pi \times 25^2 = 100.78\dots$
$= 101\,\text{mm}^2$

6 a

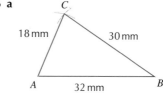

b

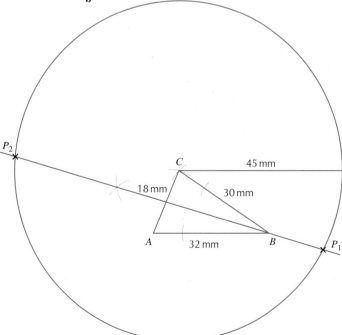

ANSWERS TO CHAPTER 5: PROBABILITY

5.1 Basic probability

1 a $\frac{2}{52} = \frac{1}{26}$ **b** $\frac{16}{52} = \frac{4}{13}$ **c** $\frac{44}{52} = \frac{11}{13}$

d P(prime) is $\frac{16}{52} = \frac{4}{13}$; P(even) is $\frac{20}{52} = \frac{5}{13}$

2 a

Number on dice	1	2	3	4	5	6
Relative frequency	$\frac{12}{120}$	$\frac{21}{120}$	$\frac{24}{120}$	$\frac{27}{120}$	$\frac{11}{120}$	$\frac{25}{120}$
	$=\frac{1}{10}$	$=\frac{7}{40}$	$=\frac{1}{5}$	$=\frac{9}{40}$		$=\frac{5}{24}$

b 20 times $\left(\frac{20}{120} = \frac{1}{6}\right)$

c No. The frequencies are not approximately equal. If it is fair the relative frequencies will all tend to $\frac{1}{6}$.

3 No. As the number is chosen at random, each number is equally likely to be chosen.

4 No. The more times the game is played, the closer the experimental probability will be to the theoretical probability.

5.2 Sample spaces and experimental probability

1 a 0.4, 0.48, 0.52, 0.56, 0.598

b Using the greatest number of trials, $0.598 \times 100 = 59.8$, giving 60 blue beads and 40 red beads

2 The sample space diagram only shows the possible totals, not the frequency with which they occur. It is not possible to say that the spinners are fair or unfair on the basis of the sample space diagram.

3 a There are more even results than odd results because of the four possible combinations, three give even numbers: odd × odd = odd, odd × even = even, even × odd = even and even × even = even.

b The probability of an even total will be less than if the dice were fair.

4 a There are 8 possible outcomes, 3 of which contain two heads. So the probability of getting two heads, in any order, is $\frac{3}{8}$.

b $\frac{1}{2}$ as third throw could only be head or tail

c 20

5.3 The probability of combined events

1 a $\frac{9}{64}$ **b** $\frac{25}{64}$ **c** $\frac{15}{64}$

2 P(prime) is $\frac{3}{6} = \frac{1}{2}$

$P(4) = \frac{1}{6}$

P(prime and 4) $= \frac{1}{2} \times \frac{1}{6}$

P(prime and 4) $= \frac{1}{12}$

3 P(red and black) $= \frac{3}{7} \times \frac{4}{7} = \frac{12}{49}$

P(black and red) $= \frac{4}{7} \times \frac{3}{7} = \frac{12}{49}$

$\frac{12}{49} + \frac{12}{49} = \frac{24}{49}$

$\frac{24}{49} \times 100 = 49\%$

The probability is **not** 50%.

4 P(not meet and not meet) is **not** $0.15 + 0.15 = 0.3$. He should have multiplied the two probabilities, not added them.
P(not meet and not meet) $= 0.15 \times 0.15 = 0.0225$

5 a i 0.28 **ii** 0.12 **iii** 0.42 **iv** 0.18

b The alternatives in part **a** together list all the different possible combinations of outcomes.

6 a ii **b** i **c** iv **d** iii

7 $\frac{1}{216}$

8 0.6

5.4 Frequency trees

1 a

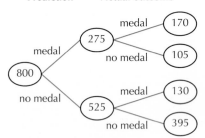

b $\frac{113}{160}$

c 21%

2 a   First part   Second part

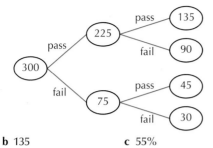

b 135   **c** 55%

5.5 Tree diagrams

1 a   First throw   Second throw

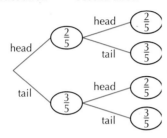

b i $\frac{4}{25}$ **ii** $\frac{9}{25}$ **iii** $\frac{6}{25}$

2 a   First choice   Second choice

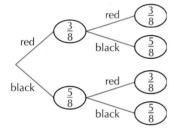

b P(same) = P(red and red) + P(black and black)

$$= \left(\frac{3}{8} \times \frac{3}{8}\right) + \left(\frac{5}{8} \times \frac{5}{8}\right)$$

$$= \frac{9}{64} + \frac{25}{64}$$

$$= \frac{34}{64}$$

$$= \frac{17}{32}$$

c $\frac{39}{64}$

3 a   First part   Second part

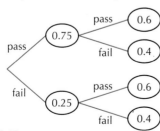

b 0.45

c P(do not pass on both parts) = 1 − P(pass on both parts)

               = 1 − 0.45 = 0.55

4 a First choice   Second choice   Third choice

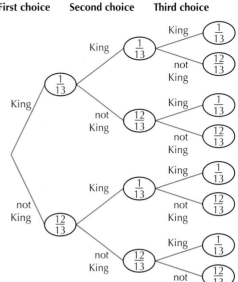

b $\frac{1}{2197}$ **c** $\frac{37}{2197}$

5.6 Venn diagrams

1 a 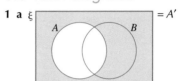 $= A'$

b 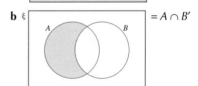 $= A \cap B'$

c 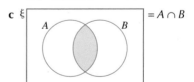 $= A \cap B$

d 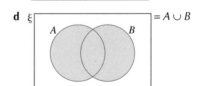 $= A \cup B$

e 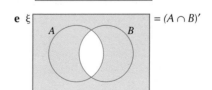 $= (A \cap B)'$

f 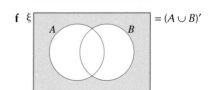 $= (A \cup B)'$

2 a ξ

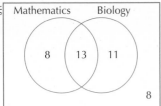

b i $\dfrac{19}{40}$ **ii** $\dfrac{8}{40}$ or $\dfrac{1}{5}$ **iii** $\dfrac{13}{40}$

3 a ξ

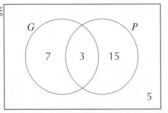

b $\dfrac{1}{6}$

ANSWERS TO CHAPTER 6: STATISTICS

6.1 Pie charts and composite and dual bar charts

1 24 people

2 a 540 people represented by 360°, so 1 person is represented by $\dfrac{360°}{540} = \dfrac{2°}{3}$.

 b $\dfrac{2}{3} \times 218 = 145.333\,333\,33 = 145°$ (to the nearest degree)

3 Although the proportion of girls and boys preferring sci-fi looks the same you don't know the number of students polled.

4 Total number of people travelling by car = 12 + 14 = 26
Total number of people travelling by all the other modes of transport = 6 + 2 + 3 + 2 +2 + 6 + 2 + 4 = 27

5 a Disagree. There are the same number of girls and boys, 47.

 b Agree

 c Disagree. The level 7 grey bar for girls is far taller than it is for boys.

 d Agree

 e Agree

6.2 Grouped frequency tables

1 a 1140 minutes

 b It is an estimate because it uses mid-class values rather than exact values.

 c 30 minutes

2 12

3 He could be correct but, as the age of the youngest and oldest are not known, other answers are possible, for example, 70 − 15 = 55.

4 Work out the total frequency (43).

 Work out the middle value $\left(\dfrac{43 + 1}{2} = 22\text{nd value} \right)$.

 Work out cumulative frequencies to decide where the 22nd value lies (5, 15, 36, …).

 The 22nd value lies in the third class (30 − 34).

5 a $a + 5 + b + 6 = 25$
 $a + b + 11 = 25$
 $25 - 11 = 14$

 So: $a + b = 14$

 b $0.25a + 5 \times 0.75 + 1.25b + 1.75 \times 6 = 25 \times 1.19$
 $0.25a + 1.25b = 29.75 - 10.5 - 3.75$
 $0.25a + 1.25b = 15.5$ (1)
 $a + b = 14$ (2)

 From (2): $a = 14 - b$

 Substitute for a in (1):

 $0.25(14 - b) + 1.25b = 15.5$
 $b = 15.5 - 3.5$
 $b = 12$

 Substitute for b in (2): So $a = 2, b = 12$.

6.3 Correlation

1 a

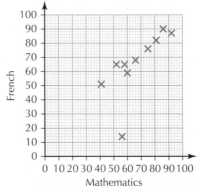

 b Strong positive: plots are almost in a line, sloping from bottom left to top right.

 c

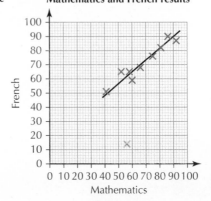

d 71–73

e Student *E*

2 a Strong positive or perfect positive correlation

b No correlation

c Positive correlation

d Strong negative or perfect negative correlation

e Negative correlation

3 a The higher the English test result, the higher the Mathematics test result.

b The greater the number of flu jabs given, the fewer people with flu.

c There is no relationship between shoe size and English test result.

d The higher the Mathematics GCSE result, the higher the Mathematics A-level result.

e There is no relationship between biscuit sales and age of purchaser.

f The higher the number of days absent from school, the lower the GCSE Mathematics grade.

4   *x* is 61 – 63

Correlation between variables 1 and 2

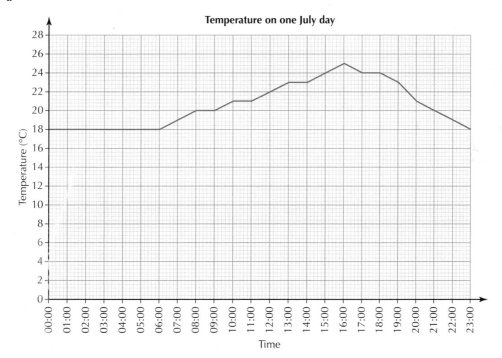

6.4 Time series graphs

1 a

Temperature on one July day

b 20.5 °C

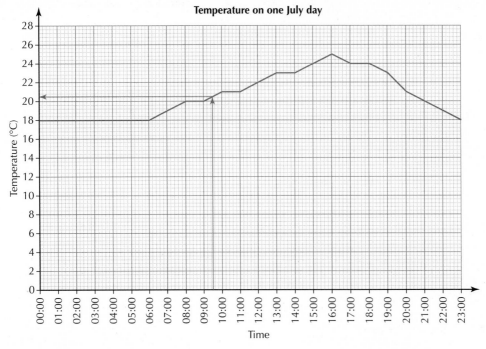

Temperature on one July day

c The temperature is static until 06:00, then it gradually increases until it peaks at 16:00, then it gradually decreases.

2 a i T   **ii** T   **iii** F

    iv F   **v** T

b Students' own choice and valid justification.

4 a No title, no label on the horizontal axis. No label on the vertical axis. Year 2007 incorrectly plotted.

b

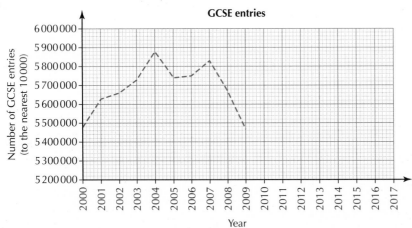

GCSE entries

The number of GCSE entries steadily increases from 2000 to 2004. It then drops slightly before peaking again in 2007, before dropping back to pre-2000 levels.

c The number of GCSE entries increases less between 2005 and 2006 than between 2000 and 2001.

3 a Over 2 000 000 visitors

b The greatest increase in number of passengers was between 2015 and 2016. This is the steepest part of the line graph.

6.5 Cumulative frequency and box plots

1 a 13 people

b 11 people

c No. The final age interval finished at age 100.

d

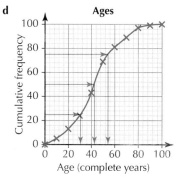

Ages

(The graph can be drawn using straight lines or a smooth curve but a smooth curve is preferable.)

e i 42–44 years old   **ii** 31–33 years old

  iii 53–55 years old   **iv** 20–24 years old

f It is making the assumption that the ages of people in each class intervals are distributed evenly across the interval, which may not be true.

2 a 50 plants   **b** 9–11 plants

  c $\frac{9}{50}, \frac{10}{50}\left(\frac{1}{5}\right)$ or $\frac{11}{50}$ **d** 12 out of 50 so 24%

3

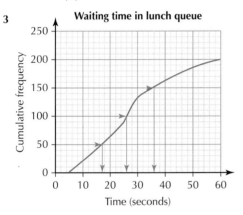

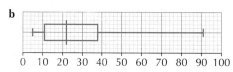

Lowest value should be 5. Median should be 26.

4 a 27 years

b

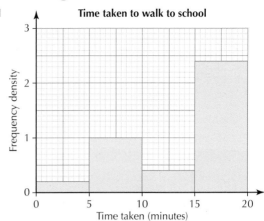

c The median for film *A* is 22 years, the median for film *B* is 35 years, so on average younger people are watching film *A*. The range for film *A* is 86 years. The range for film *B* is 36 years. The interquartile range for film *A* is 27 years, the interquartile range for film *B* is 14 years, so the ages watching film *B* are more consistent

6.6 Histograms

1

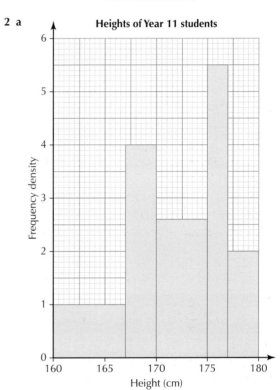

Time taken to walk to school

2 a

Heights of Year 11 students

b 11 students   **c** 4 students

3 a

Speed, s (mph)	Frequency	Class width	Frequency density
$0 < s \leqslant 15$	3	15	0.2
$15 < s \leqslant 20$	4	5	0.8
$20 < s \leqslant 25$	6	5	1.2
$25 < s \leqslant 30$	18	5	3.6
$30 < s \leqslant 40$	7	10	0.7
$40 < s \leqslant 50$	2	10	0.2

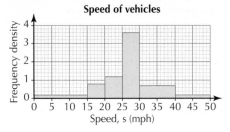

Speed of vehicles

b 40 vehicles

c 5 or 6 vehicles

6.7 Sampling

1 a This is biased. For example, the first 100 students might all walk to school.

b This is biased, as the group only includes Year 7 students.

c This is random and unbiased. Each student is equally likely to be chosen.

d This is biased, as only students who use the cafeteria are being chosen.

e This is biased, as the group only includes Year 11 students.

2 For example, uniquely number each girl. Use a random number generator on a calculator to select the required number of girls. Repeat the process for boys.

3 It is not a sensible approach as Sue needs to compare results with students who do not travel by bus with students who do travel by bus.

4 a $\frac{12}{25}$ **b** 48% **c** 36

ANSWERS TO REVISION PAPERS

Paper 1

1 $2 \times 2 \times 2 \times 3 \times 3 \times 5$ [1 mark], $2^3 \times 3^2 \times 5$ [1 mark]

2 $j = 4b$, $a = j + 18$ and $a + j + b = 72$ or equivalent [1 mark], eliminating two variables, for example, $a = 4b + 18$ with $a + 5b = 72$ to get $4b + 18 + 5b = 72$ [1 mark], solving to get ages $b = 6$, $j = 24$ and $a = 42$ [1 mark], $1 : 4 : 7$ [1 mark]

3 $\angle FDE = 128°$, corresponding angles [1 mark]
$\angle DFE = 28°$, vertically opposite angles [1 mark]
$\angle DEF = 180° - (128° + 28°)$, angles in a triangle sum to 180° [1 mark]
$\angle DEF = 24°$

4 The minute hand moves 24π [1 mark], the hour hand moves $\frac{16\pi}{12}$ [1 mark],
$24\pi \div \frac{4\pi}{3}$ [1 mark], 18 [1 mark], this is 18 so James is correct [1 mark].

5 a, b

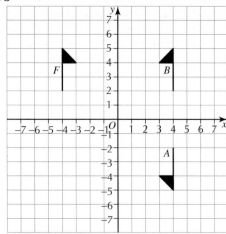

[1 mark each for **a** and **b**]

c Reflection [1 mark], in the *y*-axis [1 mark]

6 $3x + 5 = 4x - 7$ [1 mark]
    $12 = x$ [1 mark]
  $41 + 41 + y = 100$ [1 mark]
    $y = 100 - 82$ [1 mark]
    $y = 18$

7 a Gradient of first line is 4, gradient of second line is 2 [1 mark]. The gradients are different, so the lines cannot be parallel [1 mark].

b $y = 4x + n$, where *n* can be any number [1 mark]

8 $28 \times 10.5 = 294$ minutes; boys' total $16 \times 10 = 160$ minutes, $294 - 160 = 134$ [1 mark]
$134 \div 12$ (number of girls) $= 11.1666…$ [1 mark] which rounds to 11.2 minutes [1 mark]

9 £540 $\div$ 1.2 [1 mark], £450 [1 mark]

10 a $x = -2.4$ [1 mark] and $x = 0.4$ [1 mark]

b Draw the line $y = 2$ and find the points of intersection [1 mark], giving $x = -3$ and $x = 1$ [1 mark].

11 3.153   3.$\dot{1}5\dot{3}$ 3.15$\dot{3}$ 3.1$\dot{5}\dot{3}$
[2 marks all correct, 1 mark if three correct]

12 19.6×26 is approximately 20×25 [1 mark], which is 500 g [1 mark], half a kilogram, equal to *B*, [1 mark] so statue *A* must be fake [1 mark].

13 a 12 [1 mark] **b** 16 [2 marks, 1 mark for 4^2]
c 7.8×10^8 [1 mark each part]

14 £6.60; eliminating one variable, for example, 5 coffees cost £10.50 [1 mark], coffee at £2.10 [1 mark], bun price 80p [1 mark], £6.60 [1 mark]

15 a

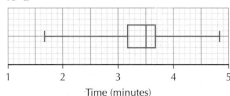

Time (minutes)

[3 marks all correct, 2 marks if 1 error, 1 mark if 2 errors]

b Any two from: Students have a greater range, students have a smaller IQR, median time higher than for teachers, the slowest student was slower than the slowest teacher, the quickest student was slower than the quickest teacher [1 mark for first correct comment, another mark for second correct comment].

16 Substitute a pair of values from the table in $y = \dfrac{C}{x^2}$ [1 mark], $C = 12$ [1 mark], $\dfrac{1}{2}$ [1 mark]

17 a $\left(\dfrac{x+3}{\sqrt{2}}\right)^2 + \left(\dfrac{x+3}{\sqrt{2}}\right)^2 = AC^2$ [1 mark],

$AC = \sqrt{\dfrac{2(x+3)^2}{2}}$ so $AC = x + 3$ [1 mark]

b $\dfrac{1}{2}\left(\dfrac{x+3}{\sqrt{2}}\right)^2 = 9$ [1 mark], simplifying this to $(x+3)^2 = 36$ [1 mark] and $x = 3$ [1 mark]

Paper 2

1 $4x + 5 = 2x + 10$ [1 mark], $4x - 2x = 10 - 5$ or $2x = 5$ [1 mark], $(x =)$ 2.5 [1 mark]

2 a $\dfrac{50^2\pi}{8}$ [1 mark], 982 cm^2 [1 mark]

b $\pi \times 100 \div 4\ (= 78.5...)$ [1 mark], $78.5... \div 3$ [1 mark], $26.179... \times 2$ [1 mark], 52.4 cm [1 mark]

3 $12 \times 30 = 360$ or 12×0.30 or 3.6 or 150 or 1.5 profit. [1 mark], $(150 \div 210) \times 100$ or $(1.5 \div 2.1) \times 100$ [1 mark], 71.4...% [1 mark]

4 a A ratio between cars with two parts correct from 2 : 1 : 6 [1 mark], all three correct [1 mark]. The ratio $(2 + 1 + 6 = 9)$ shows that the probability of a white car being next to leave the car park is one-ninth [1 mark]

5 a $x = 5$ [1 mark]

b $y = 4$ [1 mark]

c $1000^y = (10^3)^y = 10^{3y}$ [1 mark], product now $10^x \times 10^{3y} = 10^a$ hence $x + 3y = a$ [1 mark]

6 a Σxf [1 mark], total $\Sigma xf = 3285$ [1 mark], 164.25 cm [1 mark]

b Possible outliers over 175 cm skew the mean [1 mark].

7 Using Pythagoras' theorem for BC [1 mark], finding BC [1 mark], $30 - 12 - BC$ [1 mark], using tangent to find angle ABC [1 mark], 56.4° [1 mark]

8 $18.65 \leqslant x < 18.75$ [1 mark for limit on each side of x]

9 a Any of the three values 1.087(...), 0.3056(...) or 35 569(...) [1 mark], 1.8859(...) [1 mark]

b 1.89 [1 mark]

10 $\dfrac{49}{2} \div 5 = 4.9$ [1 mark], $4.9\,(5) \times £110$ [1 mark] $= £539$, which is over £500 for the week, so he is correct. [1 mark]

11 a 10 am and 10:20 am [1 mark each]

b 13×3 [1 mark], 39 km/h [1 mark]

12 $360° \div 18$ [1 mark], BCA is half of $(180° - ABC)$ [1 mark], 10° [1 mark]

13 a Although the angle is greater in Dilby, it is the area of the sector that represents the number of people with dogs and this might be greater for Chyde [1 mark].

b $P_{C\_dogs} = \dfrac{1}{4}P_C$ giving an area of 9π [1 mark]

$P_{D\_dogs} = \dfrac{1}{3}P_D$ giving an area of $\dfrac{16}{3}\pi$ [1 mark]

$\dfrac{P_{C\_dogs} + P_{D\_dogs}}{P_C + P_D} = \dfrac{9\pi + \dfrac{16}{3}\pi}{36\pi + 16\pi} = 0.2756$

$= 0.28$ (2 d.p.) [1 mark]

14 a 260×1.03^8 [1 mark], £329.36 [1 mark]

b $518 \times x^3 = 600$ [1 mark], $x = \sqrt[3]{1.1583}$ [1 mark], 5% [1 mark]

15

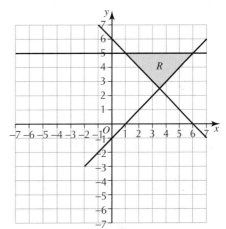

2 correct lines [1 mark], 3 correct lines [1 mark], correct region R identified [1 mark]

16 a No [1 mark]. You multiply the numbers, so there are $5 \times 10 = 50$ ways [1 mark].

b $(9 + 8 + 7 + 6.. + 1) \times 2$ [1 mark], 90 [1 mark]

17 $x = 0.764$ or $x = 5.24$ [1 mark each]

Paper 3

1 Eliminate one variable, for example, $5x = 3$ [1 mark], $x = 0.6$ or $y = 0.4$ [1 mark], $x = 0.6$ and $y = 0.4$ [1 mark]

2 Valid comparison of any two prices, for example, any two from small 0.26 p/g, medium 0.309 p/g large 0.3 p/g [1 mark]. Valid comparison of all three prices [1 mark]. Conclusion: small is the best buy [1 mark].

3 4 560 000 or 1 900 000 [1 mark], 4 560 000 ÷ 1 900 000 [1 mark], 2.4 g/cm^3 [1 mark]

4 a £2.30 [1 mark]   **b** £1.90 [1 mark]

c Σ frequency $\times$ price $\div 8$ [1 mark]; no, should be £2.025 [1 mark]

5 $0.63 \div 90$ [1 mark], 0.007 hours [1 mark], 0.007×3600 [1 mark], 25.2 seconds [1 mark]

6 336 sheep [1 mark], 126 chickens [1 mark], $378 \div 9$ (42) [1 mark], 42×5 [1 mark] = 210 cows [1 mark]

7 0.375 [1 mark]

8 5.75 cm $\leqslant$ side length [1 mark], side length $<$ 5.85 cm [1 mark]. No, it's 33.0625 cm^2 $\leqslant$ area $<$ 34.225 cm^2 [1 mark]

9 $180° \div 8$ [1 mark], so the value of x is 22.5° [1 mark]

10 240 roses in total [1 mark], $240 \div 10 \times 6$ (ratio of red roses) [1 mark] = 144 red roses [1 mark]

11 a $h = \dfrac{340}{16\pi}$ [1 mark], $A = 8\pi \times \dfrac{340}{16\pi}$ [1 mark], 170 cm^2 [1 mark]

  b Identify sides of rectangle as x and $26 - x$ and arrive at $x^2 - 26x + 144 = 0$ [1 mark], solution of quadratic as $x = 8$ and $x = 18$ [1 mark], use Pythagoras' theorem to show diagonal = $\sqrt{(8^2 + 18^2)}$ [1 mark].

12 a 2.15×10^3 [1 mark]   **b** 1.25×10^{-16} [1 mark]
  c 4.302×10^8 [1 mark]

13 a Mae, as she did most trials. [1 mark]

  b $\dfrac{88}{139} \times \dfrac{38}{139}$ [1 mark], 0.173 [1 mark]

14 a Trial and improvement, using values of 1.04^x [1 mark]; no, it will take 18 years [1 mark]

  b $40.32 - (1.2 \times 30) = 4.32$ [1 mark], $4.32 \div (1.2 \times 30)$ [1 mark], 12% [1 mark]

15 a 0.7 [1 mark]

  b Setting up $0.3 \times T < 100$ [1 mark], $T < 333.3$ [1 mark], 330 [1 mark]

16 a $110 < W \leqslant 115$ total 45 and $115 < W \leqslant 120$ total 55 [1 mark], showing these add to 100 [1 mark], yes, as this is half of 200 [1 mark]

  b $10 \times 1.6 = 16$ [1 mark], $\dfrac{16}{200} \times 100\% = 8\%$ [1 mark]

17 a 2 hours 42 minutes [1 mark]

  b Lower quartile = 2.2 hours and upper quartile = 3.3 hours [1 mark], interquartile range = 1.1 hours [1 mark], $1.1 \times 60 = 66$ minutes so Mo is wrong [1 mark]